The New Democratic Theory

KENNETH A. MEGILL

The New Democratic Theory

THE FREE PRESS, NEW YORK
COLLIER-MACMILLAN LIMITED, LONDON

The Free Press
A DIVISION OF THE MACMILLAN COMPANY
866 Third Avenue, New York, New York 10022

Collier-Macmillan Canada Ltd., Toronto, Ontario

Library of Congress Catalog Card Number: 71-122277

printing number
1 2 3 4 5 6 7 8 9 10

Dedicated to My Father

Preface

Many books are appearing which are concerned with the "disruptions" in advanced industrial society and the "unrest" which has become a normal part of our lives. Most of these books are *about* the growing revolutionary movement and speak from the perspective of the existing order. Scholars who write about radicals normally do a good job of fulfilling their roles as apologists for the status quo. Even the "sympathetic" treatments often speak in terms of agreeing with goals of the movement, but question the development of a revolutionary movement which aims at fundamental social change. The question for any radical who has found himself teaching at the university is, Must an intellectual serve the existing order, or is there some way that his work, as a scholar, can aid in the articulation of social processes now going on?

The fundamental thesis of *The New Democratic Theory* is that there is a new democratic theory emerging in both the East and the West. This new democratic theory which is developing in reaction to liberal democracy and dialectical materialism is, above all, a product of young people. Still this theory is a part of the democratic tradition. Throughout the world a new generation is developing its view of the world in a conscious and unconscious reaction to the postwar world order which was created by the cooperation of the United States and the Soviet Union. The new theory is often more a product of personal experiences and frustration with the existing order than it is a product of theoretical development. Traditional centers of learning and traditional scholars have played little role in developing the theory and practice of the movement. For this reason, the new theory appears to be a sudden appearance in the world.

Particularly in the United States the study of political subjects has been generally left to the practical politicians or the so-called empirical political scientists, and there has been little effort to study systematically the philosophical basis of democracy. At the same time philosophy in the United States threatens to become irrelevant to the world, not because it has nothing to say, but because it has forgotten how to speak to the affairs of man. It is perhaps best if philosophers remember Whitehead's dictum that what is important about a proposition is not whether it is true, but whether it is interesting. It is hoped that what is said here is substantially correct, but even more important, that it is interesting and relevant to the world in which we live.

What is called the new democratic theory is an attempt to clarify how democracy might be relevant today, but it is not merely a personal philosophical position. What is said is important and true only if it articulates the experience of a movement which actually exists and which actually has the possibility of establishing a democratic social and political order. There is a need to re-formulate our understanding of the situation in which we live in order to understand how a new kind of democracy may be possible. What is needed is not merely a description of what is happening, nor a description of what has

Preface

happened, but an articulation of tendencies present in the world which provides real opportunity for building a genuine democracy.

The theory developed here is implicit in the actions of democratic movements in many countries today. As Marx once said of another process, "They do not know it, but they *do it.*" No one book can speak for the movement, since movements speak through practical political activity. The revolutionary movement now developing is full of contradictions which are beginning to be resolved. We can speak today of a new democratic theory and a new revolutionary movement which are bringing about a democratic social and economic order.

This presentation of the new democratic theory begins historically, proceeds to a systematic discussion, and ends with a consideration of the possible strategy for a revolutionary movement. The move from concrete political and historical reality to a philosophical discussion and back to political reality is deliberate, and the work can be understood only as a whole. Any attempt to isolate the philosophical discussion from the historical context and the historical context from the philosophical discussion will lead to serious misunderstanding.

A conscious effort has been made not to use footnotes or quotations except as part of the argument. At the end of each chapter, a list of references and suggestions for further reading is given. It is hoped that the short discussions of the literature will show that the conclusions stated in the text are indicated by many of the nonradical studies of sociologists and political scientists. The suggestions for further reading include some of the major sources where the new democratic theory is being developed. Of course, there is no attempt to be complete, but it is hoped that these references will serve as a starting point for further reading. Only works written in English are included, although the most interesting information is often found in another language. It is assumed that most Americans who really read another language are already aware of the works in that language; therefore a list of foreign literature would serve no useful purpose.

One of the major shortcomings of the discussion is that the experience of only the United States and Europe is considered. This view must necessarily be warped, especially since the fight against imperialism and racism is primary today. What is shown, it is hoped, is that there are significant forces within the societies of the East and West which have an interest in fundamental social change and which will support the struggle against imperialism and racism. Perhaps even more unpardonable is the failure to discuss women's liberation at length. The women's liberation movement is clearly one of the most important forces working for a democratic society. A complete democratic theory will include the experience of the most oppressed peoples, but it is important for those of us who enjoy the privileges of the industrialized nations of the world to realize that we, too, have an interest in a revolutionary transformation of society.

Two groups, it is hoped, will find the discussion to be of value —the curious and the members of the movement. No attempt has been made to write primarily for the curious, but it is hoped that the language and argument are such that those not involved in the movement can follow what is being said. For the members of the movement, I have tried to give a general picture of what has been learned to date. All publications of the movement quickly become historical, since every advance in practice requires a re-formulation of the theoretical foundations. I hope to provide some understanding of the necessity for a close

Preface

connection between theory and practice and to give a sense of perspective for those involved in political work.

The initial conception for this book arose during a stay in Budapest, Hungary. Much of what I have written is indebted to conversations and discussions I had there. The National Endowment for the Humanities provided financial support for the study in Hungary. The University of Florida has also provided financial assistance in various ways. Many people, in several countries, read or heard various parts of the manuscript. Their comments, suggestions, and objections have been helpful. To the members of the movement who have taught me, I owe the greatest thanks.

KENNETH A. MEGILL

Contents

The New Democratic Theory

1
Looking at East-West Relations

> *The reality in the case of the United States and the Soviet Union is of two large industrial nations. Both, it has been amply shown, can achieve success by their very similar economic tests of success at the same time. Theirs is anything but implacable conflict, anything but a zero sum game as it is actually being played. . . . Both countries, quite clearly, solicit belief for what serves the goals of the industrial mechanism. Instead of contrast leading to implacable conflict, a more evident economic tendency is convergence.*
>
> J. K. GALBRAITH

For many years following World War II it was possible to speak meaningfully of an East-West power struggle and of a cold war between the free world and the communist world. Although the terminology of the cold war is still being used, the assumption that there are two power blocs in the world has recently come to be much less plausible as a basis for studying East-West relations. The unity which had been preserved around the leadership of the Soviet Union and the United States has been

Notes to this book are on pages 167–169

destroyed by changes within the two blocs. The end of the cohesiveness of the blocs has yet to produce a fundamental change in the approach which is taken to the study of the relationship of the East to the West. The underlying premise for almost all of the studies of international relations (and this is true for studies done in the East and in the West) is that there are two major kinds of social systems present in the world and that the problem of preserving peace is one of arranging a detente between the leaders of these systems.

In order for us to understand the international nature of the new democratic movement, a few prefatory remarks are necessary to clarify why a cold war analysis is no longer adequate for understanding democratic theory. Much of the new analysis of the democratic forces, both within the East and the West, depends upon a rejection of the cold war ideology and an insistence that the social order be changed. To understand the approach taken here, it is necessary to consider briefly the traditional ways of viewing political developments in the East and the West:

1. The cold war approach: There are two enemy camps. They must learn about each other in order to combat each other.

2. Peaceful coexistence approach: We must realize that neither side can destroy the other. Therefore competition will show which system is better.

3. Technocratic approach: The two sides are growing together. Economic forces are requiring the merger of the two forms of societies. Technological cooperation will overcome what seem to be ideological barriers.

It is important to notice that all of these positions are versions of a cold war doctrine. Peaceful coexistence rests upon the assumption that there are two basic kinds of societies which are

2

static and not immediately open to change. The technocrats see that there are two different societies which can be brought together by the "invisible hand" of technical development. Both the second and third alternatives are really just a development of the cold war thesis.

1. The Cold War Approach

At the end of World War II, the supremacy of the Soviet Union and the United States in world affairs led to the division of Europe into two major areas. The lines of the cold war and the lines which separate the "free" from the "enslaved," or the capitalist from the socialist, countries are exactly the lines established by Soviet and American troops. The cold war was the result of a tacit and to some extent explicit agreement of the Soviet Union and the United States to divide the territory of the world between them. Such a division required a great deal of cooperation, but the cooperation had to be accompanied by a constant claim by both sides that the enemy stood just across the line. The presence of troops in the parts of Europe occupied by the Soviet Union at the end of the war could be justified by the presence of American troops on the other side of the line. The United States could maintain its troops to control the "threat" posed by the Soviet Union. Behind these troops the societies could be changed in a manner useful to the occupying nations. Western Europe became a major outlet for American capital and a major market for American goods, while Eastern Europe provided the Soviet Union with the opportunity to develop an international economic and social system for the first time. The cold war was useful for both sides, and the ideology of the cold war—that there are two sides which must

3

treat each other as enemies—gained universal acceptance. Despite the belligerent talk, the basic agreement which ended World War II remained, with political and economic progress possible in Eastern Europe on the Soviet model and in Western Europe on the American model.

To meet the ideological needs of the cold war, in both the East and the West institutes were created for studying the enemy, with the result that a large number of intellectuals and institutions have come to have a vested interest in the preservation of the cold war. In the United States experts in Soviet Studies have been trained on the assumption that the cold war will continue in essentially the same form. Large amounts of money have been spent, both openly and secretly, by public and private groups to support the study of the enemy. In the United States students have been taught, from the elementary school through postgraduate study, that there are two basic forces in the world: the free world (good guys) and the communist world (bad guys). The propaganda problem was fairly simple—merely replace the fascists by the communists and continue to attack the "enemies of freedom." The creation of the word "totalitarian" made it possible to lump the fascists and communists together, even though they have always been bitter enemies. It was not necessary for the forces within the communist movement to be understood, but it was essential that the international communist conspiracy be fought as a threat to the "American way of life." The cold war was supported not only by the reactionary forces in the United States; the cold war policy, at least on the intellectual level, was primarily the creation of liberals who were in charge of the universities. Countless institutes and countless research projects have been approved for studying the enemy and for inventing games to determine how he can be defeated. For thousands of American

4

intellectuals the preservation of the cold war is necessary, or they will become outmoded and unemployed.

Within the communist world a similar process has occurred. A large number of intellectuals and politicians have come to have a stake in the preservation of the cold war. In the 1950's dialectical materialism was formalized and codified in textbooks, which were adopted by schools in all communist countries.[1] The dialectical materialists, like the liberals in the United States, emphasized that it was important to know the enemy. Institutes were established to study bourgeois philosophy and ideology. A generation of students (regardless of their field) was forced to learn that there are two forces in the world. In the East as in the West an intellectual machinery has been created, and thousands of teachers have been trained who would be out of a job and unfit for any other occupation if dialectical materialism were successfully attacked. The cold war is best understood, not as a war, but as a state of agreement between the liberals in the West and the dialectical materialists in the East. Both parties argue for the preservation of the status quo—for peace and order.

2. Peaceful Coexistence Approach

What appeared to be the first attack on the cold war doctrine came from the Soviet Union with the formulation of the policy of peaceful coexistence. This doctrine was formulated, not by the dogmatists, but by the liberals in the Soviet Union, who at the same time formalized and reaffirmed the dialectical materialistic position. Peaceful coexistence was based on acceptance of the fact, which had become increasingly clear, that neither side could destroy the other without being destroyed itself. In this sense, the doctrine of peaceful coexistence is

5

simply the expression of the basic assumption of the cold war policy. However, the important part of the peaceful coexistence policy was the assertion that competition would show which system is better. Peaceful coexistence served to proliferate and support the feeling that the enemy could be conquered by intellectual and economic, if not by military, means. But peaceful coexistence still assumes that the East and West are two static units, both of which are essentially stable and immune to fundamental change. In more and more areas the United States and the Soviet Union have begun to have similar purposes. An internal challenge to the social order within the various spheres of influence has become a threat to coexistence. In a sense, peaceful coexistence is just one of the theoretical ways to recognize and formalize the cold war as a permanent state of affairs.

3. Technocratic Approach

Another position which still operates within the framework of the cold war position has become particularly popular among the "reasonable" men in both the East and the West. This position accepts the fact that the basic social relationships are given by the post world war settlement and that there will be no significant economic or political changes within either bloc. The technocrats see the problem of improving East-West relations as a technical problem, which can be solved only if it is stripped of all ideology. Ideology is dead, it is claimed, and even if we understand that the other side must occasionally use the language of its ideology, we know that it does not take it seriously. By furthering technical contacts and realizing the mutual self-interest in preserving the current world order, it is supposed that most of the significant problems can be solved and tensions can be reduced.

6

The contacts and cultural agreements between the East and West are a logical outgrowth of this view. It may not be possible for politicians to benefit much by talking with each other, but actors, physicists, and even sociologists and economists can benefit by mutual contact. For the East, these contacts provide a way for certain individuals to achieve technical training, which is important in the developing economies of Eastern Europe. For the West, these programs provide the hope that a "goulash communism" will emerge, in which the communists will become fat and happy and therefore not be dangerous. The assumption is that the dangerous people are those who disturb order—the order supported by the liberal theory in the West and dialectical materialism in the East.

The technocrats point to the basic tendency toward decentralization in all European communist countries and toward concentration in the Western countries. They rightly point out that the traditional language of socialism and capitalism conceals the fact that a very similar kind of decision-making process exists in both systems. But they conclude from this fact that the problems of East-West relations can be overcome by technical improvements, if we only realize that ideology is a mirage which needs to be ignored so that we can get on with the practical work. The technocrats, with their solution of practical work, rather than apparently useless ideological debates, would doubtless be correct if the social orders were essentially stable.

4. The Beginning of a New Democratic Theory

For the new democrats, democracy will be possible only if there are fundamental changes in the social and economic

7

relations within both East and West. They reject the basic assumptions in all three forms of the cold war doctrine: that the societies in the East and West are essentially stable and will remain unchanged.

It is not surprising that the revolt in many parts of the world has been interpreted as a mindless opposition to the current order, for it cannot be understood within the liberal and dialectical materialistic categories. The western liberal interprets the democratic forces inside communist countries as primarily working for liberalization—for the creation of a liberal political system which is better adapted to an industrialized society.

The myth of a cold war between the United States and the Soviet Union has served primarily as an excuse for repressive measures against the revolutionary movements within the existing order. So-called communists are punished in the West, and revisionists are punished in the East. The leaders in the East and West fail to notice that the revolt is not in favor of the other side, but is against the established order. This failure to understand the true nature of the revolt sometimes leads to very comical situations, such as when the communist press publishes a story praising the Italian or American students for demonstrations while condemning Polish or Czech students for their demonstrations or when the American liberal press treats the Polish or Czech students as "freedom fighters" and condemns its own students as anarchists, who are destroying the very fabric of a reasonable society. The new democratic theory strikes at the heart of the cold war agreement when it calls for revolutionary transformation of the existing order. Those in revolt today do not look with longing to another society, but begin with a critical analysis of the situation in which they live.

Undoubtedly the ruling forces in both the East and West are more adept at seeing danger within their own countries than

8

they are at understanding events in other parts of the world. The fact that the revolt is part of a general movement for the establishment of a democratic social order has been overlooked. The new democratic theory which is beginning to emerge in many different situations and in many different parts of the world is not only a response to local conditions, but is also the beginning of a new theory of the nature of a democratic political and social order.

The revolutionary movements in the East and the West have already shaken the postwar arrangement. The war in Viet Nam has shown that certain parts of the world have refused to understand what the cold war game is all about and have begun to play by rules written neither by the liberals nor by the dialectical materialists. It is not surprising that the liberals within the United States and the dialectical materialists in the Soviet Union have tried to understand even the war in Viet Nam according to the rules laid down by the cold war agreement. The Secretary of State does not speak of "communists," but of the "north" or simply of the "other side." The communist authorities speak simply of the "aggressors." The conflict in Viet Nam has shown that the lessons which have been taught by the sovietologists in the West and the dialectical materialists in the East have failed when the two blocs are confronted with a situation in which the cold war agreement is challenged. Social forces in much of the third world, which are not aligned with either bloc, have shown that neither the United States nor the Soviet Union can claim to be masters of the world. The revolutionary forces of the world, with which the new democrats of the industrial nations identify, are looked upon as being among the strongest forces working to destroy the old order.

Since World War II all nations have claimed to be democratic, at least on paper. Immediately after World War II the

Red Army installed peoples' democracies in Eastern Europe, and the American dollar established capitalist, liberal democracies in Western Europe. When India won independence, one of the world's largest democracies was created, using England as the model for representative democracy. In the United States the social reforms begun by Roosevelt were accelerated, and the New Deal became the Fair Deal. In England, social reforms which had been delayed for decades were rapidly brought about by a socialist government, and British imperialism began to come to an end. In Central Europe, the Soviet model was forced on all countries as drastic social and political changes were introduced, and the old aristocratic power structure was destroyed. In the first years after the end of World War II it looked as if democracy had really come of age. Immediately after the war in both the East and the West, those who called themselves democrats were in control.

It is difficult to remember the hope for democracy which was once present. In Asia and Africa, government after government has been overthrown by the military, and true independence has yet to be won. In Eastern Europe, except for a few months of hope in 1956 and 1968, Stalinism has been strong, and a democratic development appears to be, at best, a process which will take many years. The United States, once thought to be the leading advocate of democracy, entered a dirty war far from home, which can best be understood as an act of imperialistic aggression. The United Nations reports that the developing countries of the world are losing their fight for subsistence and are not increasing their production rapidly enough even to keep up with the rising population. Everywhere, what once looked like the golden age of democracy has turned out to be an illusion.

References

We continue to speak of democracy. Yet if even half of the current gloom is justified, there seems to be little reason to hold that democracy has life as a movement and as a theory just at the moment when those who called themselves democrats engage in brutal wars in order to "save" their democracy. Democracy seems to be little more than a farce, whether it is the democracy in the East or in the West.

To understand the development of a new conception of democracy, it is necessary to understand why the two major democratic theories have failed. In the following chapters we shall focus primarily on the development of democratic forces in Hungry and in the United States. A similar treatment of the new theory could be made, with some changes, if we were to consider the democratic movements in other Eastern European countries and the radicals of Western Europe. It is in reaction to particular situations that we must understand how a new kind of democratic theory and democratic movement is possible today.

References

FLEMING, D. F., *The Cold War and Its Origins*, Doubleday, New York, 1961, two volumes.

> A massive and detailed discussion of the cold war until 1960. Fleming argues that the cold war could not have been won and shows how its effect was to solidify and fortify the two sides.

GALBRAITH, JOHN KENNETH, *The New Industrial State*, Houghton Mifflin, New York, 1967.

> An influential member of the liberal community, Galbraith has demolished many of the economic myths of the liberal theory. In this book he sets out to show that the development of technology is bringing the Soviet Union and the United States closer together.

HOROWITZ, DAVID, *Empire and Revolution*, Random House, New York, 1969.

> A radical interpretation of contemporary history, which shows the relationship of capitalism to the cold war and the development in the Soviet Union. A selected bibliography is included which indicates other sources for looking at contemporary history in a radical way. Horowitz has also written and edited other books which show that the cold war does not at all have the character we have been led to believe.

LAFEBER, WALTER, *America, Russia, and the Cold War*, Wiley, New York, 1967.

> A historical account of the cold war, which argues that "domestic policy influences foreign policy." No general ideological discussion is given, but the book does provide a compact historical guide to the period and includes an extensive bibliography.

MAGDOFF, HARRY, *The Age of Imperialism*, Monthly Review Press, New York, 1969.

> A study of the American empire and the necessity for expansion of the American economic system. One of the best economic treatments of the nature and scope of American imperialism.

MORRAY, JOSEPH P., *From Yalta to Disarmament: Cold War Debate*, Monthly Review Press, New York, 1961.

> A treatment of the cold war as a "contest between ideologies." One is left with the feeling that the discussions were ideological, as Morray claims, but were not nearly so important as he argues, because the ideology appears to be made more for internal consumption rather than for any international effect.

OGLESBY, CARL, and SHAULL, RICHARD, *Containment and Change: Two Dissenting Views of American Foreign Policy*, Macmillan, New York, 1967.

> Oglesby's discussion is one of the earliest treatments by the New Left of the imperialistic nature of American foreign policy. Although the optimistic and humanistic elements of the book would no longer be shared by most of the movement, it is still a classic of the movement. Oglesby sums up the central question as: "Whether or not Americans will choose to be free is the transcendent political question, the one question that coordinates and subsumes all searching issues of foreign and domestic policy. If Americans choose freedom, there can be no totalitarian America, and without a totalitarian America, there can be no American empire" (p. 164).

References

REAGAN, MICHAEL D., *The Managed Economy*, Oxford University Press, New York, 1963.

> Reagan sets out to destroy the myth that the United States has a free enterprise economy and ends by calling for more centralized planning. As he concludes his book, "democratic planning, under Presidential direction, is freedom's visible hand" (p. 267). Although no radical conclusions are drawn, the discussion does bring together the results of an impressive number of social and political scientists, which show clearly that the liberal democratic theory has little relationship to the reality of the United States. In the end, however, he has merely moved to a social democratic position and has not challenged the basic American theory or reality.

WELLS, DONALD A., *The War Myth*, Pegasus, New York, 1967.

> A warm and well-reasoned argument for the pacifist positioh by a man who has been active in the resistance to the draft movement. Although Wells's arguments are scarcely accepted in the movement today, the pacifists were the first to begin to oppose the war in Viet Nam and were dominant during the early stages of the movement.

2
Learning
to Be Radical

The chief end [of civil society] is the preservation of property.
J. LOCKE

Democracy in the United States and Western Europe is understood as a system in which a representative government is elected and controlled by the majority in such a way that the rights of minorities are protected. Social disputes, according to this liberal democratic theory, are resolved by integrating minorities within the system. With integration it becomes possible for minorities to participate in the electoral process, through which decisions are made. The liberal democratic theory is a democratic theory because the people are able to control their fate through elections, but in order to do so they must enter into the bargaining process which goes on among the various minorities.

The development of a radical political theory in the United States has come not from the educational and academic institutions, but began as a practical reaction to discrepancies within the liberal society. Only recently has there begun to be a theoretical discussion to accompany the revolt against the liberal democratic theory. For several years, even though students and faculty members have been involved during their free time with the problems of civil rights and the war in Viet Nam, involvement in political affairs has seldom been carried into the classroom and research room, where a theoretical understanding of the failure of the liberal society could be investigated. Radicalism in the United States has had to be learned, not at the university, but in the process of trying to solve particular problems within the existing order which claims to be democratic.

Two practical issues united the democratic forces in the United States and served as a learning process for the new democrats. The civil rights struggle and the organized opposition to the war in Viet Nam have created a large number of young people who are disillusioned with the society in which they live and who have made practical efforts to bring about by persuasion changes in this society. It is precisely because persuasion has failed that the movement has developed from a pressure group demanding certain specific and minimal changes within the liberal democratic framework to a movement demanding fundamental changes in the social and economic system of the United States. The new democrats learned to adopt a position opposed to the prevailing social order only after the order had been tested and found to be wanting.

The summer of 1964, known as the Mississippi Summer, stands as the high point of enthusiasm for liberal democracy and is also the decisive moment when those who had become involved in the struggle for civil rights for the Negro began to realize that the liberal democratic society could not provide genuine freedom for him. The strategy guiding the activity during the early days of the civil rights movement was obvious to all Americans imbued with the ideals of liberal democracy.

Learning to Be Radical

In Mississippi, and elsewhere in the South and North, the problem was thought to be simple: The blacks had not been allowed to vote; therefore if the fundamental rights of voting and access to public schools on an equal basis could be guaranteed, then all other necessary social changes would follow. Indeed, if democracy *means* the right to vote, then the securing of the vote was all that would be required for the institution of democracy. The task of the Mississippi Summer was to bring the blacks in the South within the political and social life of the United States. The project was welcomed by the liberals throughout the nation, and the enthusiasm among the singing, chanting workers was contagious for the whole country. There seemed to be hope that democracy really could be meaningful for the blacks, if only the right to vote could be won.

Several years and many elections later the failure of the strategy adopted in Mississippi has become obvious. Even though the number of black voters has increased considerably, there has been no significant improvement in the lot of the blacks. The election of a black to even a local office is still a major news story.[2] The Southern racist senators, who have consistently killed or modified attempts at federal action to aid the blacks, are still chairmen of powerful committees. They still claim to represent states with large Negro populations.

If anything, the blacks have become even more alienated from society and are even more impoverished economically than before the liberal strategy was adopted. The civil rights struggle is dead, and instead the battle for black power in the cities of the North has begun; no one seriously holds that the strategy of the Mississippi Summer can provide the slightest hope of solving the problems of the blacks in the ghetto. Democracy conceived as a system of electoral politics has shown itself to be a farce for a substantial portion of the population.

Learning to Be Radical

It has become obvious that only fundamental economic and social change can begin to meet the problem of the lack of freedom for the blacks in the United States.

Black power has become the theoretical expression of the realization that liberal democracy is bankrupt. Disorder in the cities has been the spontaneous, unorganized, and undirected expression of the realization on the part of the blacks that the liberal democrats cannot help them to gain control over their lives. Black power expresses clearly that revolution and power are necessary for a genuine freeing of the blacks. The panic-stricken reaction of the liberal democrats shows that the message of black power has been understood. Not integration, but the development of genuine integrity for the local community and power for all human beings to organize and plan their own lives is at the heart of black power. Community control can be developed only if the property relations which support the liberal democratic institutions are fundamentally altered. In short, black power is one of the first genuinely revolutionary theories to develop in the United States.

At first, black power was little more than a slogan, but it was a slogan which captured the failure of liberal democracy and began to provide the direction for a movement away from liberalism. Concretely, black power means local organization, new political institutions, and economic independence for the black community and also the development of the specialness of the black. The whites are told to work for their own freedom in their own community but to realize that they are responsible for the centuries of oppression of the blacks. Freedom requires the creation of a whole new set of political and social institutions, which are separate from the white power structure. An independent police and judicial system is already developing in black communities as it has been realized that the police and judicial system organized by the elected representatives can neither provide protection nor give justice to the people who live in the ghetto. The day-to-day life in the ghetto has come more and more under the rule of habit and informal pressure, rather than the rule of the white establishment. During the first rebellions in the ghettos it was understood which buildings should be burned down and which areas should be attacked, thus showing that even in moments apparently the most unorganized of all, there existed a set of genuine social institutions and customs that operated where the white man's police failed. The law and order of "whitey" failed, but a new kind of law and order was revealed.

Economic independence is the most important goal for the black man. The most significant part of the black power position is its focus on the oppressive economic system, which is supported by the liberal democratic theory. In the attempt to create new social and economic institutions, the black power advocates have insisted that these institutions be under community control. A kind of socialism absent from the American tradition is being established in the center of certain American cities. As the black power movement developed it was realized that in order to achieve genuine community control over the economic institutions, it was necessary to free the ghetto from outside interference and to bring about democratization in the economic affairs of the nation at large. For black power to be real, there had to be a change in the white community as well. The liberation of the blacks presupposes the liberation of the whites from racism and an unfree society.

There have been some attempts to organize the poor white community along the lines suggested by black power, but they have not been notably successful. The black revolution will continue to be led by the blacks. The success of the democratic

19

movement in the United States will largely depend upon the ultimate victory of the black revolution and the successful creation of revolutionary movements in the ghetto, which can serve as examples for the rest of society. Because of the particularly open nature of the oppression of the blacks, they are beginning to develop radically new institutions more rapidly than the unorganized whites.

Had it not been for the war in Viet Nam, perhaps the black revolution could have been quickly suppressed, and a massive program of federal expenditures could have relieved the worst pressures on the black community. Perhaps many of the racial problems in the United States could have been solved within the framework of liberal democracy. Liberalism is a theory that has always argued for formal freedom from oppressive institutions. The original aim of the poverty program was to bring the black population within the liberal middle-class society and ideology. Had it not been for the war in Viet Nam, this strategy might well have succeeded, and black power would never have developed into an important revolutionary movement.

The failure of the Mississippi Summer project and similar liberal efforts to integrate blacks into white society and to bring about a genuine democratization produced the first wave of radicals in the United States who have expressed their rejection of the liberal theory by the black power argument. In 1968 a similar process of radicalization with regard to the Viet Nam war took place. In late 1967, Eugene McCarthy announced his candidacy for the presidency, with the expressed purpose of bringing the protest against the war and those engaged in these protests within the political system. The McCarthy campaign, particularly in its early stages, was an attempt to integrate a minority into the political system of the United States. Particular policies (such as the conduct of the war in Viet Nam) were questioned, but there was no discussion of the nature of the American society which had produced the war in Viet Nam. The McCarthy campaign mobilized thousands of people, particularly young people, and gave them hope that they could have a place within the political system.

Like the Mississippi Summer project of 1964, the McCarthy campaign of 1968 failed to integrate the protesters into the society and produced instead a new generation of radicals. The radicals of 1968 were made by the failure of the traditional political machinery, which the liberal theory and the liberal society claimed was adequate to make any necessary change. By the time the Democratic Convention was held in Chicago it had become clear to an increasing number of people that it was impossible for the war in Viet Nam to be brought to a close by working within the social and political institutions present in the United States. Even more important, a large number of people had begun to ask why the war could not be stopped and what caused the American society to participate in an imperialistic war in a far-off country. What began as an integration process turned out to be a radicalization process for a significant part of the population. By the end of the Chicago convention many McCarthy sympathizers understood that the system itself, and not merely a particular policy, needed to be attacked.

The final act of the McCarthy campaign, appropriately enough, took place in the streets, not in the convention hall, which had been established by the political authorities as the place where political decisions ought to be made. The police action against the demonstrators and the McCarthy campaign workers showed clearly that the United States governmental system rests ultimately on force and that if necessary this force will be used to suppress a movement which aims at changing the social and political system of the United States.

The failure of the final attempt to end the war in Viet Nam through the political process radicalized a large number of people and showed that the disillusionment with the existing order had become widespread. The new democrats have been created as they have tried to go through the existing channels, which are supposedly offered for changing the liberal society. The breakdown of the liberal ideology and the disillusionment with the liberal society have created the possibility for a genuinely new democratic theory to begin to develop.

The war in Viet Nam is a classic example of a war fought to "save" democracy and preserve the American sphere of influence. It began as a small police action supposedly designed to protect the rights of another country to remain free and to prevent the "international communist conspiracy" from a victory won by military means. Just as the events after the Mississippi Summer showed that racial problems cannot be solved with the framework of liberal democracy, so the past few years have shown that the war in Viet Nam is not against external aggression, but instead is being waged by the United States in order to protect its economic and political position in the world.

In the minds of the younger American generation, for the first time, the United States has clearly been on the wrong side in a war. This astounding fact has sent many young people back to the history books, and under a critical eye, the un-emphasized imperialistic nature of the American political tradition has begun to emerge. The war in Viet Nam, to those who have looked again at the history of the United States, is no longer viewed as an isolated tactical mistake, but is seen as the most flagrant and obvious act of imperialistic aggression by a mighty nation with a long history of imperialism against smaller nations in Latin America and Asia. After repeated revelations concerning the role of the secret police (CIA) of the United States in the internal affairs of many nations and disclosures that the secret police have dominated many domestic organizations as well, little faith remains in the current order, which claims to be democratic. The loss of faith in the ability of the present government structure to provide a democratic order has perhaps been the most important result of the war in Viet Nam. The failure of liberal democracy in both the racial situation and in Viet Nam has revealed that a new way of understanding democracy is necessary if the problems of racial injustice at home and imperialism abroad are to be met. Just as the blacks have discovered that freedom will not come to them until the economic structure of the white community is altered, so the opponents of the war in Viet Nam have come to understand that there must be a fundamental change in the social and economic structure before wars such as that in Viet Nam can be eliminated.

While the development of the new democratic forces in the United States has been the result of the practical experience of seeing the collapse of the accepted institutions of society, the theoretical rejection of the liberal democratic theory, which was the basis for the social order in the United States, is only now being formulated. The significant fact is that merely the formulation of the premises of the liberal theory is almost sufficient to refute the theory itself. The problem is not to *refute* the liberal democratic theory, but to *portray* it and to show that it is meaningless—that it is simply irrelevant as a theory for a democratic society today.

It is generally held that liberal democracy is based upon two major principles: majority rule and minority rights. Undoubtedly the first principle is that the majority rules. In an assembly, whether it be the United States Congress, a ladies league for better schools, or any other small or large group, the assumption is that an organization is democratic if the majority rules. An important corollary to this principle is that in any sizable group, it is impossible for the majority to decide all matters directly; therefore, responsibility must be delegated. Parties, factions, and groups are built within the organization and play the most important role in decision making. In practice the principle of majority rule means that there must be at least two parties within a democratic organization or state and that these two parties must alternate in holding power; it must be possible for the party in power to be replaced. The principle of majority rule thus holds that a nation or organization is democratic if there is a possibility for the party in power to be replaced and if minorities can be integrated into the system.

The second crucial principle for the liberal democratic theory is that there are certain rights of the individual which cannot be violated. Even a majority cannot take them away from individuals and groups within the organization or state. Examples are freedom of speech, of the press, of assembly, of religion, and (traditionally) the right to property. Individual rights must be protected in order to leave the possibility open for new parties and other collectivities to be formed which can replace the party in power.

It would, however, be misleading to conclude that liberal democracy means only that the majority rules and that the rights of individuals are protected. Equally important is the presence of a capitalist, or so-called free enterprise, economic system. Majority rule and minority rights are required as principles for political organizations if the capitalistic economic order is to function well. John Locke emphasized that the natural rights of man apply not only to individuals, but to private property as well, and he described the purpose of the liberal democratic government as being to protect private property. According to Locke, the individual, in order to protect his property, enters into a civil society, that is, a society which is ruled by laws. A state, a political power, is created to protect property, which includes man's life and liberty. In order to determine who rules, man must allow the majority to make political decisions, as long as the rights of property are not infringed upon. Since the purpose of government is to protect property, government has no right to infringe upon the property created by an individual.

The liberal theory of democracy, which received its classical formulation with Locke, links majority rule, natural rights, and private property. The ordinary understanding of democracy in the United States today is basically Lockean, and his conception of democracy is still repeated in most civics textbooks. It is important to notice that several assumptions are necessary if this view is correct in connecting majority rule, individual rights, and private property:

1. Man is, essentially, an individual who owns property.

2. Man can, by and large, determine what is in his best interests through an act of will, such as voting.

3. In order for man to act politically, political parties must be created which can express the will of the individuals in society.

All these assumptions necessary for the liberal democratic theory have been challenged since Locke wrote. Almost no one, whether he be a philosopher, a political scientist, or the man in the street, would seriously argue today that man is *essentially* a property-owning animal. Furthermore, the notion of man having a "will," through which he can directly and rationally express what is in his best interest, has also been widely rejected as being too simple-minded to be taken seriously as the foundation for a theoretical work. The will has proved to be notoriously difficult to locate, and almost all contemporary philosophers and scientists would reject a theory requiring man to have a will which he can express in a direct, rational manner.

The third fundamental assumption of liberal democracy, that political parties can express the will of individuals through the election process, has been the one most thoroughly investigated by empirical political scientists. Although this assumption is only one of the necessary elements of the democratic theory put forward by the liberals, it is the one assumption which can be more or less empirically tested. If it could be shown that it is possible, through the party machinery and voting, to control one's fate and protect one's property, then we would have to conclude that the liberal theory is at least an adequate, generalized description of an existing political system, even if we would not want to accept it on other grounds. However, from the studies made of voting behavior in liberal democratic societies, it can be concluded that the election mechanism does not provide a way by which the individual can control the political authorities. In political decision making, the results of the electoral process play a modest role. Public policy is primarily determined by the interests of the dominant economic class.

The importance of the discovery that the creation of a "fair" voting system does not ensure control of the government by the people has been largely ignored in the discussion of the nature of democracy. Almost all of the democratic movements in the United States at the beginning of this century were chiefly concerned with the introduction of direct democratic processes

—such as initiative and referendum, where indirect procedures had been in effect—and with broadening the right to vote to include all segments of society. The political scientist Dahl has perhaps best expressed the conclusions of those working within the liberal democratic theory by stating that

> We cannot correctly describe the actual operations of democratic societies in terms of the contrasts between majorities and minorities. We can only distinguish groups of various types and sizes, all seeking in various ways to advance their goals, usually at the expense, at least in part, of others. . . . A good deal of traditional democratic theory leads us to expect more from national elections than they can possibly provide.[3]

While realizing that the principle of majority rule has never functioned as the liberal theory has contended, Dahl does not question the liberal theory. Instead, he speaks of an "American hybrid," which he insists "is not for export to others."[4] At best, the democratic theory articulated by political scientists such as Dahl is a peculiarly American phenomenon, which cannot be exported to others and serves as a justification for the continuation of the capitalistic economic order in which those who control the property play the most important role in fixing public policy. Dahl and other liberal democrats begin with the assumption that the United States is democratic. The results he presents in his work reflect this assumption and constitute an ideology rationalizing and justifying the current political order. Unless parties can express directly the will of individuals, then the liberal democratic theory, at least in its traditional formulation, is no longer valid. Almost no one would today hold that the liberal theory is still adequate, either as an accurate description of the political process or as a proposal for reform; however, as an ideology—as a way to understand our political life—the liberal theory of democracy is still predominant.

Learning to Be Radical

The concepts of majority rule and minority rights fail to provide us with an adequate way of understanding the nature of democracy in an advanced industrial nation. They have become part of an ideology which supports the existing order and obscures the fact that man does not have control over his life and the society in which he lives. The practial and theoretical experience in the United States have shown that the liberal democratic theory can be taken seriously only as an ideology which supports the existing social and economic forces. It fails both as a way of understanding the current order of society and as a theory for a movement set on establishing a new democratic order.

The collapse of the liberal democratic theory as an adequate theory of democracy has also meant that the economic system based upon this theory cannot provide a democratic social order. The new democrats in the United States have a new theory of democracy because they understand that a change in the social system, and not merely a change in personnel, is necessary for there to be democracy. One of the most important tasks for the new democrats is to gain control of the economic system. Unless some kind of effective public control of the economic order can be established, a solution of the racial and military problems in the United States does not seem to be possible. Private ownership of the means of production exists best in a society dominated by a liberal theory of democracy. The new democrats in the United States have been radicalized and have begun to understand that only an economic system under public control can serve as the basis for a democratic political order.

References

BACHRACH, PETER, *The Theory of Democratic Elitism, A Critique*, Little, Brown, Boston, 1967.
> Although hampered by anticommunism and timidity, which keep him from taking a radical position, Bachrach does give a good criticism of the liberal democrats who have dominated the field of "political theory." His own solution ("modern self-developmental" theory) is hardly grounded, but his criticism of others shows the dead end of contemporary political theory, at least as a theory of democracy.

BARBOUR, FLOYD B. (ed.), *The Black Power Revolt*, Extended Horizons Books, Porter Sargent Publisher, Boston, 1968.
> Perhaps the best collection of writings on the development and content of the Black Power concept in its early years. An extensive bibliography is included.

BURDICK, EUGENE, and BRODBECK, ARTHUR, *American Voting Behavior*, The Free Press, Glencoe, Ill., 1959.
> A collection of articles on voting studies. Eugene Burdick, "Political Theory and Voting Studies," develops the contradictions present in many of the studies between their theory and their conclusions and even indicates tentatively that there is a need for a "radical reorientation by political theorists" (p. 149). This statement, made before the movement began its own criticism, is a further indication of the failure of the traditional liberal democratic theory.

CAMPBELL, ANGUS, CONVERSE, P. E., MILLER, W. E., and STOKES D. E., *The American Voter*, Wiley, New York, 1960.
> An exhaustive and exhausting summary of voting research, which concludes that the electorate "is almost completely unable to judge the rationality of government actions" (p. 543). The claim is made that electorates influence "broad policy," but the entire assumption is that the capitalist system is permanent and the United States is "democratic" by definition. The book shows clearly that empirical research destroys the liberal theory; yet no conclusions which are counter to the prevailing system are allowable.

CARMICHAEL, STOKELY, and HAMILTON, CHARLES V., *Black Power: The Politics of Liberation in America*, Random House, New York, 1967.
> A discussion by the first person to popularize and formulate the concept of Black Power.

Learning to Be Radical

DOMHOFF, G. WILLIAM, *Who Rules America?*, Prentice-Hall, Englewood Cliffs, N.J., 1967.

> Domhoff shows that there is a governing class in the United States and that this class includes a small group of people who control business and government power structure. Although Domhoff does not give a radical analysis of movements opposing the ruling class, he does show that government exists in the United States to protect property.

DOMHOFF, G. WILLIAM, and BALLARD, HOYT B., *C. Wright Mills and the Power Elite*, Beacon Press, Boston, 1968.

> A collection of reviews and criticisms of C. Wright Mills's *The Power Elite*, a book which first raised, on a broad scale, serious doubts about the American "democratic" system. Mills played an important part in making radical thought a part of the American discussion.

FAGER, CHARLES E., *White Reflections on Black Power*, William B. Eerdmans Publishing Co., Grand Rapids, Mich., 1967.

> A discussion by a sympathetic white of the importance of Black Power. Particularly good for its bibliography and for its attempt to present the argument in a systematic way to a white audience.

HENTOFF, NAT (ed.), *The Essays of A. J. Muste*, Bobbs-Merrill, Indianapolis Ind., 1967.

> A collection of essays by the single most important pacifist theorist. Muste articulated and formulated the theories of civil disobedience which were an important part of the early civil rights and antiwar activity.

HOLT, LEN, *The Summer That Didn't End*, Morrow, New York, 1965.

> The summer did end, but this more or less "official" history of the Mississippi Summer of 1964 is still important. Of particular interest is an extensive appendix of documents.

JACOBS, PAUL, and LANDAU, SAUL, *The New Radicals, A Report with Documents*, Random House, New York, 1966.

> Contains many of the early documents of the movement.

KENNISTON, KENNETH, *Young Radicals*, Harcourt, New York, 1968.

> A sympathetic study by a psychologist of the workers involved in the "Vietnam Summer" of 1967. Kenniston effectively destroys the prejudice that radicals are social misfits. He also shows the disappointments which led those opposed to the war in Vietnam toward a consciously radical perspective of society in general.

References

KILLIAN, LEWIS M., *The Impossible Revolution? Black Power and the American Dream*, Random House, New York, 1968.

> Killian gives a basically sound history of the development of black power as a revolutionary slogan. He treats the racial question in isolation from other movements which are present, but he does recognize the fundamental challenge to the system which the black movement now presents. A good, short bibliography is included.

MALCOM X, *Autobiography*, Grove Press, New York, 1964.

> Perhaps the most important autobiography for understanding the way in which the black man comes to political consciousness. Malcolm X was a true leader of the black political movement and was one of the first to understand its revolutionary implications.

PETRAS, JAMES, and ZEITLIN, MAURICE (eds.), *Latin America: Reform or Revolution? A Reader*, Fawcett, Greenwich, Conn., 1968.

> An excellent collection of articles on Latin America, which show the way in which the United States is imperialistic and discusses possible ways in which imperialism can be combatted. Of particular interest is the class analysis of Latin American society.

PRESTHUS, ROBERT, *Men at the Top, A Study in Community Power*, Oxford University Press, New York, 1964.

> A study of two community power structures, which concludes that "despite high levels of popular education, economic stability, a fair degree of social mobility, a marvelously efficient communication system, and related advantages usually assumed to provide sufficient conditions for democratic pluralism, the vast majority of citizens remains apathetic, uninterested, and inactive in political affairs at the community level. Most political scientists and sociologists who have analyzed community behavior accept this generalization" (pp. 432–433). The apathy, however, is not seen by Presthus to be a result of the existing structure.

Report of the National Advisory Commission on Civil Disorders, Bantam Books, New York, 1968.

> Even a group of liberals appointed by the President had to conclude that the United States is a racist society and that the blacks live in an intolerable situation. The conclusions are weak, but the description of life in the black community is moving.

Learning to Be Radical

SUTHERLAND, ELIZABETH (ed.), *Letters from Mississippi*, McGraw-Hill, New York, 1965.

> A collection of letters from volunteers in the Mississippi Summer Project of 1964. The letters show that contact with the problems of the blacks pushed many whites in a more radical direction and showed them that much more than voter registration was needed.

ZINN, HOWARD, *Vietnam, The Logic of Withdrawal*, Beacon Press, Boston, 1967.

> A well-written little book which argues that the United States should withdraw from Vietnam. Zinn's book played an important part in molding opinion against the war.

3
Democratic Marxism

What is now happening to Marx's teaching has, in the course of history, happened repeatedly to the teachings of revolutionary thinkers and leaders of oppressed classes struggling for emancipation. . . . After their death, attempts are made to convert them into harmless icons, to canonize them, so to say, and to surround their names with a certain halo for the "consolation" of the oppressed classes and for the purpose of duping them, while at the same time emasculating the content of the revolutionary teaching, blunting its revolutionary edge and vulgarizing it.
LENIN

In the preceding chapter the process of radicalization in liberal democratic society has been traced. Becoming radical is a commonly accepted course for a young man or woman to take. The blacks, students, and some younger professionals have rejected the order which claims to be democratic and are faced with the problem, What is my relationship to tradition, and how do I understand my own position in relation to that of others? In most of the Western countries the radicals have been turning to the Marxist tradition for an alternative to the liberal theory. In the beginning they were perhaps only reject-

33

ing the anticommunism which has been an important part of the liberal theory, but more recently the renewed interest in Marx and Marxism has made a development of a radical theory possible again. At the same time in Eastern Europe a return to Marx has been used to develop a radical consciousness. In both East and West radicals meet on one common ground: an insistence that Marxism, the authentic Marxism, be taken seriously.

But the questions immediately arise, What is authentic (democratic) Marxism? How can a radical accept what is presented as Marxism by the leaders of the Soviet Union? What is the genuinely democratic Marxist tradition? The theoretical formulation of Marxism which is generally considered to be orthodox was developed in the Soviet Union and given the name *dialectical materialism*. This term does not appear in Marx's writings, and it was not until the twenties that dialectical materialism was presented as a comprehensive theory which could explain all social and natural phenomena. One of the earliest formulations of some of the essential elements of dialectical materialism was made by Nikolai Bukharin in *Historical Materialism*. In this work Bukharin tried to develop a system of sociology and to provide a systematic view of Marxism which would be adequate for a situation in which Marxism was to be the dominant and official philosophical position. Bukharin's formulation was widely attacked by Marxists as being too dogmatic and failing to encompass the richness of the Marxist tradition. Of particular note are the criticisms of Gramsci and Lukacs.[5] In the end, largely because Stalin used the full political power of the state to stop all theoretical work in the Soviet Union and to enforce an official version of Marxism, the crude and comprehensive statement of Marxism was generally accepted as orthodox Marxism.

The attempt to formulate a unified science was not unique to the Marxists in the twenties and the thirties, but in the Soviet Union this unification was brought about by political force, rather than as the result of scientific investigation and discussion. The formulation of dialectical materialism was completed in the late fifties, after Khruschev asked for intensive theoretical work in his speech to the Twentieth Party Congress (1956), in which he also denounced Stalin. As a result of this request, a series of textbooks were written by committees, which became the official statement of dialectical materialism. Perhaps the tone of these books can best be illustrated by the authoritative statement that there are three basic laws of the dialectic: the law of the unity and conflict of contradictions, the law of transformation of quantitative into qualitative changes, and the law of the negation of the negation. These three laws, plus many others that were enunciated, were supposed to explain all social and natural phenomena.

The official dialectical materialism was widely disseminated in all countries where communist parties loyal to the Soviet Union were in power. It is important to note that the final and most dogmatic formulation of dialectical materialism was accomplished by those who were "liberalizing" the political system.

Despite the attempt to preserve unity, dialectical materialism has come under heavy attack, and the attempt to present Marxism as one unified theory has already been abandoned in fact if not in word. Discussions of the nature of logic, the status of Marx's early writings, the status of social laws, and the relationship of particular sciences to dialectical materialism—all have resulted in making dialectical materialism increasingly abstract in attempting to maintain its position as the scientific philosophy which can serve as the basis for all other sciences.

35

As dialectical materialism has become increasingly abstract, it has become meaningless and uninteresting. Contradictory propositions are adopted, and both are called a part of the doctrine. Widely varying interpretations have grown up in each of the socialist countries, and yet the claim is still made that dialectical materialism is essentially unchanged. During this process, the theory has not been refuted; it has simply become a meaningless position, with all the horrors this phrase once had for an analytic philosopher. Dialectical materialism has ceased to dominate philosophical life in Central Europe, and it has been relegated to an ideology used in official pronouncements, just as traditional liberalism has been largely relegated to an ideology to be used in official pronouncements defending actions of Western governments.

One of the major tasks of any new formulation of democratic theory must be the rediscovery of the authentic Marxist tradition. Much of the discussion in the East European countries has centered on the problem of the correct interpretation of Marxism. In later chapters we shall consider some of the particular content of this discussion, and in the next chapter we shall look at one example of a Marxist who has kept the faith within the authentic Marxist tradition. The reemergence of democratic Marxism comes at a time when a new democratic movement is being developed. Dialectical materialism has failed as a democratic theory precisely because it has lost all contact with the democratic movement. The genuine advance over liberalism of even such a poor formulation of Marxism as dialectical materialism ought to be recognized, but the authentic Marxist tradition must be rediscovered if the new democratic theory is to be correctly formulated. The refusal to accept dialectical materialism as an authentic Marxist position is not to be equated with anticommunism. On the contrary, dialectical materialism is better viewed as a regrettable deviation from the genuine revolutionary communist position.

In the West it has been generally understood that dialectical materialism is not now a democratic theory. The social democratic parties have claimed that Marx's analysis is outdated, and they have rejected his theories as a basis for their present political programs. Throughout the social democratic tradition they have understood democracy in the liberal sense and have considered liberals to be their potential allies. Eduard Bernstein, the founder of social democracy, said that social democracy was the "legitimate heir" of liberalism "not only in chronological sequence, but also in its spiritual qualities, as is shown moreover in every question of principle in which social democracy has had to take up an attitude."[6] For Bernstein and the social democratic tradition the task of socialism was to "organize liberalism."[7] Of course the social democrats rejected laissez-faire capitalism and argued, at least initially, for state ownership of the means of production, but they never called into question the liberal theory of democracy. The relationship of man to his work and of man to his political institutions were to be in the liberal tradition.

Since the liberal tradition in the United States led naturally into Roosevelt's New Deal, the connection between social democracy and liberalism was kept even in the language which was used. After World War I most European liberal parties, on the other hand, were replaced by social democratic or labor parties, and in several countries the social democrats controlled the government. In America, the liberals preserved their name and consciously maintained their links with the liberal tradition, while adopting the economic policies of the European social democrats. American liberals and European social democrats continue to understand democracy as a political

Democratic Marxism

system in which majorities rule through representatives and the
rights of minorities are protected.

The problem of the social democrats (and the liberals in the
United States) has been how political power could be gained
rather than how a revolutionary change could be made. In
country after country the social democrats have come to
power or have shared power with other parties. In the process
the link with the Marxist tradition has been consciously broken,
and Marx is relegated to being a more or less important forerunner of social democracy, as a man who had a good moral
conscience, but who failed to predict correctly the outcome of
capitalism. The social democrats and the liberals have accepted
the capitalistic economic order as their own and have found
that by organizing liberalism their aim could be gained—
they have come to power within the liberal democratic system.
It is precisely against the tradition of liberalism and social
democracy that the current radical movement in Western
countries has grown up. In order to get at the real Marxist
tradition it is necessary to reject social democracy and its
liberal understanding of the nature of democracy.

Lenin correctly attacked the liberal tendencies in Marxism
and insisted that the authentic Marxist tradition was a revolutionary one. The problem for Lenin and other authentic
Marxists was not to seize control of the state, but to smash the
state apparatus and to create a new social order. The authentic
Marxists have insisted that a new way of life—a new social
order—must be created before genuine democracy can be
achieved. As long as the revolution stops short and revolutionaries are willing to accept political power within the system
rather than continue to demand a genuine democratic society,
they will fail to develop a movement which will create a new
form of society.

The democratic Marxists are not those who have chosen

38

reform within the current order, nor are they those who have chosen to play the game according to the rules declared by the liberal democrats. The social democratic movement which has attempted to "revise" Marx in order to "bring him up to date" has almost always fallen into the trap of giving up hope for any fundamental change in society in favor of short-range political power within the liberal democratic order. These Marxists see Marx as an important forerunner of contemporary sociology and economics, but not as the founder of a revolutionary theory. They have done little more than adopt the liberal democratic theory as their own. Those within the Marxist tradition who have given up their authentic position (loyalty to the revolutionary movement) in an attempt to become acceptable to the liberals have agreed with the liberal theory that democracy means rule through elected officials. These so-called non-dogmatic Marxists have found their place primarily within the bureaucracy of the trade union movement and the political parties. The authentic Marxist insists that democracy must mean the possibility of all institutions being brought under the control of those who live and work in them; in order for this to happen a revolutionary transformation of the economic and social order is necessary.

The authentic Marxist tradition is radically different from the social democratic tradition, which saw itself to be the logical heir of liberalism. These Marxists attacked not only the symptoms of capitalism, but its form of economic organization and the liberal democratic theory as well. For these Marxists, revolution is a necessary and important part of social life. The revolutionary movement must be based on real social forces, which can be mobilized to seize control. Loyalty to the democratic movement, not seizure of power for its own sake, is the primary characteristic of the authentic Marxist.

The democratic elements within Marxism can be traced to

two major sources: Marx's theory of communism as true democracy and Lenin's understanding of the party revolutionary
praxis as a means of bringing about fundamental social change.
The Marxist viewpoint is in several respects superior to the
liberal democratic theory. Within Marx's philosophy much of
the utopian and liberal tradition is reinterpreted in social,
rather than individual, terms. The working class, by far the
largest in the nineteenth and early part of the twentieth century, was seen by Marx as the potential source of a revolutionary
movement, which would change the social order to make democracy possible. That the movement did not develop in exactly
the manner which Marx conceived is not as important as the
fact that he and later Marxists understood democracy to be the
rule of the working class. Marx's theory of democracy as the rule
of the proletariat is a genuinely democratic theory, for it describes the way in which the people can control their own fate in
a modern society. The Marxist theory was the first to emphasize
that to be a democracy, the society must be one in which man
has control over his working situation, and it was also the first
theory to understand the democratic movement in terms of
historically important economic forces and not merely in terms
of the ideas of particular thinkers. The Marxist method,
which combines a theory of history with a theory of social
organization, is still the best one for understanding the new
form of democracy today.

Lenin's theory of a revolutionary party, through which power
can be achieved and the old order destroyed, was an important
addition to the democratic theory of the rule of the proletariat,
as developed by Marx. It was Lenin who correctly interpreted
Marx and who succeeded in leading the first explicitly Marxist
democratic revolution. The Leninist theory of revolutionary

activity understands revolution as a product of conscious activity. He correctly understood that democracy, at least in most of the world, can be achieved only if existing state and social structures are destroyed. Piecemeal changes in a country without a democratic tradition can bring about no significant social change.

Before World War II the orthodox Marxists were successful in only two revolutions: in Russia in 1917 and in Hungary in 1919. The Hungarian revolution was crushed within six months, but the Russian revolution, despite the attempt by outside forces to destroy it, survived a civil war and was able to bring about fundamental changes in the Russian society. Accordingly, the authentic Marxists in the twenties recognized Russia as the single example of a successful revolution. Although since that time the Western world has denied the essentially democratic character of the Russian revolution by dwelling upon the appearance of bureaucratic Stalinism in the late twenties, to the radicals, in both the East and the West, the discussions among the Marxists in the twenties are a good example of a free and open development of the Marxist position.

Under the leadership of Marxists who had gained power by revolutionary means, the Soviet Union successfully caught up with the industrialized nations of the world. This accomplishment must be recognized as at least partially a result of the power of Marxism, even in the form it later assumed in the Soviet Union under Stalin. That this catching up was not merely an accident has been shown by the successful industrialization of Central European countries which came under the leadership of Marxist parties after World War II. No matter how much one may oppose the brutality of the Stalinist methods (and one can oppose Stalinism and still be an authentic Marxist), one must recognize that the nations of Central Europe have become a part of the industrialized world. This great accomplishment has been possible only because the traditional aristocratic and semifascist governmental and social order in Central Europe was smashed. The Marxists democratized a large part of Europe, not by introducing liberal freedoms, but by destroying an outdated and undemocratic order.

The success of Marxism, even in the form it took in Central Europe, has raised new problems, which resemble those faced by Marxists in the liberal democracies. In order to move beyond a process of merely catching up to the industrialized world, the nations under Marxist control must complete the creation of economic and political democracy. Since the major means of production are already in public hands, it is possible for society to be democratized. Yet even though the successful socialization of the economy has established a base for democratization, this democratization can be carried out only if the authentic Marxist tradition can be revived and a practical alternative to dialectical materialism created.

If democratic Marxism is understood as the theory which is loyal to the revolutionary movement, then the democratic forces in Central and Eastern Europe are best understood as radicals, rather than as liberals. In early 1968 the radical forces gained control of the party and political apparatus in Czechoslovakia and began to build a democratic socialist order for the first time in history. It would be a grave mistake to see the Czech experiment primarily as a liberalization in which the "oppressed peoples" attempted to "free" themselves. There were virtually no demands for a return to capitalism, and the term "democratic socialism" was widely accepted.

The importance of the Czech experience in the development of a new democratic theory and society must not be underestimated. Since the shortlived experiment is unique and since there are virtually no historical precedents, it is difficult to give real content to the phrase "democratic socialism," which was adopted by the Czech radicals. Theoretical and practical difficulties were compounded by the fact that there had been relatively little theoretical work done in Czechoslovakia, because political and intellectual oppression had continued almost to the very time when the change in government took place. The phrase "democratic socialism," like "Black Power" in the United States, has served to express dissatisfaction with the current order. In addition, it has pointed the direction in which a new democratic order must develop, by emphasizing the importance of staying within the tradition of revolutionary socialism, which was first formulated by Marx.

It is easy for Americans to emphasize how the democratic theory of Marxism was warped and distorted by the party when it came under the control of Stalin. In the twenties there were many communists—including Lenin, toward the end of his life—who were aware of the dangers present in the bureaucratic structure which took control of the party. The question of the proper organization of the communist party was at the center of the Marxist discussion at that time, but the so-called democratic centralism, which became accepted, did not allow any real discussion or contact with the revolutionary movement. The organization of a revolutionary party after the seizure of power is crucial for the development of a democratic social order, and in all Marxist countries where democratization has been pursued, this issue has been the focus of discussion. The party which was based on the Leninist model was successful in seizing control in a revolutionary situation, but failed as an instrument for thoroughgoing democratization of society, at least as it was developed under Stalin. Nevertheless, the concept of the party as an organization which understands the nature of history and works for revolutionary change can still be valid despite the fact that Stalin was able to use a revolutionary party to create a tyranny in the name of democracy.

The democratic Marxist tradition is not to be found among those who have given up their revolutionary position in order to work for minimal gains within a basically capitalistic order. Neither is it to be found among those who have claimed to be the orthodox Marxists under Stalin and his successors. Both the Stalinists and the liberal democrats have diverted democracy from its basic tradition of the rule of the people to a rule of political parties, either in a pluralistic multiparty system or in a one-party system. The "people" have been replaced by the "party," and the party has been understood as those who control the party organization. The democratic Marxist, like any new democrat, must take democracy in its most radical formulation and understand the democratic system as one in which people are able to control their lives.

The problem of discovering a democratic Marxism is at least partly one of delving into the history of Marxism to understand what went wrong during the Stalinist period. A new democratic theory emerging out of the Marxist world must explain what happened to the Marxist tradition in the hands of the one-party rule when the party was controlled by Stalin. Just as the new democrats in the liberal democracies are constantly called upon to face oppression at home and imperialism internationally, so the Marxists, who are seeking to build a new democratic order, are called upon to face both the remaining influence of the Stalinist system and the imperialistic actions by the Soviet Union in preserving its own sphere of influence. But the democratic tradition in Marxism need not be rejected in the process. During the discussions among the

Marxists in the 1920's, the authentic Marxists were opposed to both the growth of the party bureaucracy under Stalin and the attempt by Stalin to turn Marxism into an ideology used to further the interests of the Russian state.

Democratic Marxism is authentic Marxism—the Marxism which emphasizes the necessity for revolutionary action. Loyalty to the movement, not loyalty to any particular doctrine, is characteristic of the orthodox democratic Marxist. In the following chapter we shall take the example of one man who has sought to maintain his loyalty and to participate in the democratic movement over a long period of time. The Hungarian Georg Lukacs has been an important theoretician and political figure for fifty years. In order to come to a further determination of the essential characteristics of authentic Marxism, we shall look at his work and the sense in which the new democratic forces in Central and Eastern Europe stand in the democratic Marxist tradition.

References

American Institute of Marxist Studies Newsletter. Available from AIMS, 20 East 30th Street, New York, N.Y., 10016.

> A bimonthly newsletter which includes a bibliography of works on Marx and Marxism. One of the most valuable sources of information on Marx scholarship and new works in the Marxist tradition.

APTHEKER, HERBERT, *The Nature of Democracy, Freedom and Revolution*, International Publishers, New York, 1967.

> A nice little book by the leading theoretician of the Communist Party, U.S.A. Aptheker has kept alive much of the tradition of Marxism and has shown that communism can still be an American product.

BARAN, PAUL A., and SWEEZY, PAUL M., *Monopoly Capital*, Monthly Review Press, New York, 1966.

> Perhaps the only contemporary economic analysis of capitalism by American Marxists. This book has been one of the most influential books in the movement.

Democratic Marxism

BOCHENSKI, J. M., *The Dogmatic Principles of Soviet Philosophy*, Reidel, Dordrecht, Holland, 1963.

> A synopsis of one of the official Soviet texts on the fundamentals of Marxist philosophy which contained the theory of dialectical materialism.

BUKHARIN, NIKOLAI, *Historical Materialism*, University of Michigan, Ann Arbor, 1969.

> A translation of Bukharin's book which tried to present a system of sociology in 1921.

DEGEORGE, RICHARD, *The New Marxism, Soviet and East European Marxism Since 1956*, Pegasus, New York, 1968.

> More a catalog of issues and positions than a theoretical discussion, the book does show that the "official" position of dialectical materialism is under heavy attack. The book suffers from being an objective study by a sovietologist who has little sympathy for Marxism.

DEWEY, JOHN, *Liberalism and Social Action*, Capricorn Books, New York, 1963 (first published 1935).

> Dewey is perhaps America's best example of a social democrat, and his impact has been decisive on the "liberals" from Roosevelt through Johnson. In this little book he clearly describes how the tradition of liberalism must develop into what could best be called a social democracy in order to be adequate. Through Dewey's influence, the liberal tradition was transformed into a social democratic position in the United States, while keeping the name "liberal."

Monthly Review. An Independent Socialist Magazine.

> One of the most stimulating journals of Marxism and socialism. The monthly magazine also includes news and analysis of the movement throughout the world.

PETROVIC, GAJO, *Marx in the Mid-Twentieth Century*, Anchor Books, New York, 1967.

> This little collection of essays is one of the first attempts to work out a post-Stalinist philosophical position. Petrovic, a Yugoslav, is the editor of *Praxis*, an international journal on Marxism, which has been of great importance in rediscovering the Marxist tradition. The book could be attacked from many angles and is now of more historical than theoretical interest, but it is still one of the few systematic attempts to go beyond dialectical materialism.

46

References

SOMMERVILLE, JOHN, *The Philosophy of Marxism, An Exposition*, Random House, New York, 1967.

> An exposition of dialectical materialism, which includes questions and dogmatic answers at the end of each chapter. This book is the closest thing in English to the textbooks on dialectical materialism which have traditionally been required reading for all students in Central Europe and the Soviet Union.

ZEITLIN, IRVING M., *Marxism: A Re-examination*, Van Nostrand, Princeton, 1967.

> Perhaps one of the best summaries of the Marxist position. Written by an American sociologist who tries to work out in what sense Marx was a scientist.

4
An Example of Authentic Marxism

The teachings of Marx must daily and hourly be re-worked and assimilated on the basis of praxis.
G. LUKACS

The anticommunism into which almost any American has been indoctrinated may make it somewhat difficult for him to conceive of Marxism as a theory to be identified with a genuine democratic tradition. To make the nature of authentic Marxism clearer, we will deal in this chapter with the position of an authentic Marxist, Georg Lukacs, who during a long career has kept his loyalty to the revolutionary movement while preserving his theoretical and personal integrity.

The interpretation of the life and development of Lukacs presented here is not universally shared. Particularly among West European social democrats it is popular to characterize Lukacs as a philosopher who repeatedly changed his position in order to avoid conflicts with the authorities. In this book it is held that this is an erroneous interpretation. Lukacs has not been an "official" philosopher at any time. The development of his position has to be related to developments which have taken place within the revolutionary movement. Although it is not our intention to give a full account of the life and activity of Lukacs, an initial summary will serve as a basis for the discussion. Then, by reviewing some of his theoretical contributions to Marxism, we shall try to come to an understanding of the authentic Marxist tradition.

Lukacs was born in 1885 in Budapest and studied in Hungary, where he received the doctor of philosophy degree in 1906. In 1909 he began his long association with German philosophy and heard lectures in Germany by the *Lebensphilosoph* Georg Simmel. Beginning in 1913, Lukacs worked closely with Max Weber, Emil Lask, and Ernst Bloch. By 1915 Lukacs had already written three major works: *Die Seele und die Formen* (The Soul and the Forms), *Entwicklungsgeschichte des modernen Dramas* (The History of the Development of the Modern Drama), and *Die Theorie des Romans* (The Theory of the Novel). Beginning in 1915, Lukacs again took an interest in Marx, whom he had previously considered to be a social scientist whose works had to be divorced from his revolutionary activity. After returning to Hungary in 1917, he became increasingly involved in the radical movement. In 1918 Lukacs joined the newly formed Hungarian Communist Party and began to play an important role in the political life of Hungary. Within five months after the party's founding, a Soviet republic was established in Hungary; from March through August 1919, Lukacs was its assistant minister and then its minister of education. He also served as the political commissar of the Fifth Red Division. Although the revolutionary government lasted only six months, it was a historically important attempt to install a democratic communist government in Hungary. Lukacs, through his participation in this government, gained practical political experience and involvement, which came to play a decisive role in the subsequent development of his philosophical position.

After the fall of the revolutionary government Lukacs went into exile in Vienna. There, only the intervention of leading European writers and intellectuals, such as Thomas and Heinrich Mann, saved him from being returned to Hungary, where he would almost certainly have been executed.

During the 1920's Lukacs played an active role in the Communist Party. In 1923 he published a collection of essays entitled *Geschichte und Klassenbewusstein* (History and Class Consciousness), which established him as one of the leading theoreticians of the democratic movement. In this work he combined his philosophical training and political experience to provide brilliant discussions of the problems of organizing the workers movement and the nature of orthodox Marxism, a criticism of Kant, and a discussion of the concept of alienation, which was later discovered to be an important part of Marx's philosophy when the early writings of Marx were published in 1932. The political and philosophical writings of Lukacs have been very influential and controversial; throughout his life he has been attacked for some of the positions he took in this book, and he has modified much of what he said. Nevertheless, it is still considered to be one of the classics in the history of Marxist theory and even today exercises considerable influence, particularly among the people of Western Europe who are seeking a non-Stalinist Marxist tradition.

Between 1933 and 1944 Lukacs lived in the Soviet Union, where he devoted himself primarily to literary critical works and the problems of aesthetics. In 1944 he returned to Hungary with the Red Army and became a member of parliament, a member of the governing body of the Hungarian Academy of Science, and professor for aesthetics and philosophy of culture at the University of Budapest. Only after his return to an official position was it possible for him to publish the great body

51

of his literary and critical philosophical works. Politically, Lukacs continued to emphasize the importance of uniting socialism and democracy. By 1949 he was once again in difficulties with the political authorities and in 1951 was forced to withdraw from political life. Lukacs played an important role in the events leading to the uprising in 1956, and in that year he began his open and strong attack on Stalinism. In October of 1956 he became a member of the Central Committee of the Communist Party and was briefly the minister for education in the Nagy government, which was forcibly removed when the Russian troops entered Budapest. Along with other members of the government, Lukacs was deported to Rumania. He was allowed to return to Budapest in April 1957 but was dismissed from the Communist Party, removed from his university post, and forced into retirement.

Although Lukacs was already known throughout the world as the author of *History and Class Consciousness* and as a literary critic and theoretician of literature, nevertheless, at the age of seventy-two, he began a new and important phase of his philosophical life. The new leisure Lukacs had after returning to Budapest allowed him to continue with a project he had first planned in 1912—a systematic aesthetics, which would eventually contain three parts. In 1963 the first of the parts was published as a two-volume work, *Die Eigenart des Ästhetischen* (The Characteristics of the Aesthetic). This is a part of his collected works, which is eventually to contain fifteen volumes and is being published in West Germany. The aesthetics is not only the summation of a lifelong project for Lukacs, but is the beginning of a series of philosophical works of the kind which were repressed during the years when dialectical materialism was the official Marxist position. Before completing the other two parts of the aesthetics, Lukacs hopes to write an ethics and what he calls an ontology of social life.

Lukacs has written most of his major works in German (they have only later been translated into Hungarian) and has made his Marxist philosophy a part of the international philosophical life. His return to systematic philosophy has once again opened the possibility for the discussion of Marxism as a living and vibrant position. Throughout his life Lukacs has worked for a Marxist philosophy of high quality. In all periods of his life he has been a source of inspiration to his associates, and he has sought out and encouraged others to do good theoretical work in the Marxist tradition. Despite his repeated difficulties with the Party organization, Lukacs has maintained his connection with the democratic tradition in Marxism and with the revolutionary movement. Even today he has considerable knowledge of the student movement in the West, with which he is critically sympathetic. He has remained a genuine radical, and his position has grown and developed throughout his life.

In the fall of 1967 Lukacs was readmitted to the Communist Party—ten years after his request for readmission—and since that time interviews with him have been published in which he has called for fundamental democratic reforms. The development of philosophical life in Hungary since the war is largely a product of the presence of Lukacs. He has shown by word and by deed that Marxism need not be identified with Stalinism.

The life of Lukacs is an example of personal and theoretical involvement in the democratic movement; it further expresses the continuity of authentic, or democratic, Marxism. Many of the leading democrats in this century were also communists. Some of them have had constant difficulties with Stalinist governments. These democrats, like Lukacs, did not break with the Communist Party or with Marxism, but worked within the Party for democratization. The new democratic theory in Central and Eastern Europe will emerge from these democrats, who have understood Marx as a philosopher who saw the possibility for a genuine democracy in an industrialized nation.

In recent years the opposition to Stalinism has been the chief tie which has bound together the new democrats in Central and Eastern Europe. The initial reaction to Stalinism after Stalin's death produced a momentary political force which demanded a relaxation of the most oppressive police-state tactics and the creation of conditions which would allow at least the minimum of free expression. The struggle for minimal security was won, and it would be unwise to picture Central Europe as a group of countries living under an oppressive dictatorship, in which all decisions are imposed by an external force. Often, however, de-Stalinization has not meant a fundamental change in the Party and other political organizations. The new democrats, who were initially united around programs for civil liberties, now understand their role as being to bring about a consequent democratization. As in the United States, they are focusing their attention on the problem of creating democratic institutions. They also understand that civil liberties will become meaningful only when new institutions are created which allow fundamental decisions to be made democratically.

It is difficult today, when Marxism sometimes takes on a dogmatic and sterile form, to imagine how important and stimulative was the discussion within the Marxist movement in the twenties. Marxism was understood, not as a fixed dogma which could be relayed to future generations, but as a method of analyzing historical events and as a theory for understanding the possibilities for developing genuinely democratic institutions. In 1923 Lukacs expressed—in the essay, "What Is Orthodox Marxism?," which was included in *History and Class*

An Example of Authentic Marxism

Consciousness—what is perhaps the very opposite of the Stalinist view of Marxism:

Orthodox Marxism does not mean a critique-less acceptance of the results of Marx's investigations; does not mean a "belief" in this or that thesis; does not mean the interpretation of a "holy" book. Orthodoxy in the question of Marxism refers much more, finally, to the *method*. It is the scientific conviction that in dialectical Marxism the correct method of investigation has been found and that this method can only be developed and deepened in the sense of its founder. However, all attempts to go beyond Marxism or to "improve" it, have only led to and must lead to simplification, triviality, and eclecticism.[8]

Or, as Lukacs was to explain in a short autobiography which he wrote in 1933 "The teachings of Marx must daily and hourly be reworked and assimilated on the basis of praxis."[9] And finally in 1956, at a speech before the Petöfi Circle, Lukacs pointed out that Stalinism had done one of its greatest injustices by preventing the development of an authentic Marxism:

The tremendous historical guilt of Stalinism exists in the fact that not only was scientific development not followed up, but this development went backwards. Stalin hindered just those tendencies which would have been capable of developing Marxism.[10]

The break with Stalin, according to Lukacs, must not be understood merely as a return to liberal democracy. The new democrats are still within the Marxist tradition, which dominates the intellectual life in Eastern Europe. The break with the Stalinist form of dialectical materialism must be a "radical break"[11] that realizes that "with Stalin it is in *no way*—as many wanted us to believe for a long time—a matter of *occasional particular mistakes*, but it appears as a false system of observations (*Anschauungen*). . . ."[12] The radical break with the false system of Stalinism is an act within the Marxist tradition and begins with the recognition that Stalin only stood at the top of a pyramid "which consisted of always smaller Stalins."[13] The radical criticism of Stalin and Stalinism, such as that made by Lukacs, points clearly in the direction of a new democratic theory. Only if Stalinism is recognized as a systematic perversion of the democratic and authentic Marxist tradition can the construction of a democratic theory begin.

In an interview printed in the Party newspaper, shortly after his readmission to the Party in 1967, Lukacs insisted that any true reforms, which would bring about democratization, must be regarded as a definite break with the past and not merely as technical improvements in an essentially democratic social and political order.

This would be correct if we dealt here purely with a question of technology or business administration, and not something vastly more important. The emphasis on evolution alone necessarily entails the suppression of the principles involved in the change. Do not misunderstand me, I am not saying that everything has to be changed by tomorrow, but I do believe that if we do not fight resolutely and tenaciously for the change then things will not be changed over the years either. The young Hegel produced the following witty paradox: "if we wish to *change* something, then *something* has to be changed." I am fighting so that the superstructure will be changed as soon as possible. The clearer the masses see what it is all about, the sooner they will progress beyond the old.[14]

By insisting that reforms ought not to be seen merely as slight improvements, Lukacs emphasized the importance for Hungary both of self-criticism and recognition that fundamental social problems still have to be met.

In the short passages by Lukacs cited, there are two important conceptions which must be part of any democratic Marxist theory and which are important in the new democratic theory: The first is the negative conception that Marxism is not a belief or dogma. It is not a set of propositions to which one must subscribe in order to be accepted. The effects of the dogmatic

interpretation of Marxism, which was widely accepted in both
the East and the West, have been devastating, both in countries
which claimed to be Marxist and in societies which rejected
Marxism for the wrong reasons. To say that Marxism is not a
dogma does not mean that it must be "improved." Those who
have wanted to go "beyond" Marxism by adopting the
liberal position have, in the end, given up all hope of fundamental social change.

The second, positive, conception is that of *praxis*. It is in
returning to the concept of praxis that the possibility for the
development of a genuinely democratic Marxism exists. Marx
expresses his notion of praxis in his famous third thesis on
Feuerbach:

The materialistic doctrine concerning the change of circumstances
and education forgets that circumstances are changed by men and
that the educator must himself be educated. . . . The coincidence of
the change of circumstances and of human activity or self-change can
be comprehended and rationally understood only as revolutionary
practice (praxis).[15]

For an American, perhaps the Marxist notion of praxis can
best be explicated by contrasting it with the conception of the
practical. To be practical, one attempts within any system to
solve problems arising within that system. The practical man
knows how to use the rules of the game to his advantage. He
takes what is given and then attempts to modify his behavior
and the behavior of others to produce the most "rationally"
organized society and social order. To be practical, one plays
the game and understands and abides by the rules prescribed
by the existing social order. Through praxis one also learns what
ought to be done and develops his strategy. Praxis, however,
unlike practice, is revolutionary in form. The man of praxis is
revolutionary; the practial man takes the given social order as

permanent. The man of praxis is not always practical. He understands that in history—in man's life as a social being and as an individual—there are genuine leaps and qualitative changes. To learn from praxis is to develop a revolutionary doctrine which will enable one to understand the basic forces in history and the possibilities for developing a revolutionary movement so that men may gain control over their lives. It is not sufficient merely to solve problems within the existing forms of society.

The authentic Marxists—the democratic Marxists—understand that we do not control our own fate simply by relying on wishful thinking; on the contrary the possibility for creating a new society rests upon man's ability to make his own history. As Marx put it:

> Men make their own history, but they do not make it just as they please; they do not make it under circumstances chosen by themselves, but under circumstances directly encountered, given and transmitted from the past.[16]

A democratic theory which is part of the authentic Marxist tradition emphasizes that man can really change the conditions in which he finds himself only if he is a part of a revolutionary movement. Such a movement can be successful only if it is based on objective forces in society, and not on a vague utopia. The creation of a new world takes place in a situation which is presented to man, and man's activity can be meaningful only in relationship to "circumstances directly encountered, given and transmitted from the past." Democratic Marxism is a philosophy of praxis. It must be a philosophy which emphasizes the possibility of finding a movement, present in the world, which can create a new world. Not merely a slightly refined version of the old world, but a genuinely new world, is the goal of a revolutionary movement. For the authentic Marxist the

An Example of Authentic Marxism

possibilities for revolutionary change lie in changing the nature
of the social order and in bringing about a fundamental change
in property relations. A philosophy of praxis—a genuine
authentic Marxism—must, as Lukacs said, constantly rework
its theory and learn to understand the current situation.
But the current situation is understood so that the forces available for creating a new society can be understood.

The Marxist conception of praxis is based on Marx's description of work in *Capital*:

Labour is, in the first place, a process in which both man and Nature
participate, and in which man of his own accord starts, regulates,
and controls the material re-actions between himself and Nature.
He opposes himself to Nature as one of her own forces, setting in
motion arms and legs, head and hands, the natural forces of his
body, in order to appropriate Nature's productions in a form
adapted to his own wants. By thus acting on the external world and
changing it, he at the same time changes his own nature.[17]

For Marx, and for advocates of any real Marxist position, work
is a process of exchange, in which both nature and man undergo
change. It is the fundamental activity of man's life. In an
advanced stage of society, such as that found in industrial
nations, work has become a highly socialized process and can
proceed only through cooperation. Indeed, much of Marx's
discussion in *Capital* is a presentation of the historical development through which cooperation has become more and more
important for the working process. If Marx's definition of work
is not understood and the fact that the working process is now
a social process is not understood, then Marx's insistence that
the working class is the basis of the new democratic community
will not be understood. The socialization of work has proceeded
beyond that described by Marx. The working class needs to be
more broadly defined than was the case in the nineteenth

59

century, but the criterion for determining its members remains the same: A worker is a socialized man who changes nature and in the process is changed.

The authentic Marxists, unlike the "practical" liberals, understand work as a process in which the world is changed and not merely adapted to. The characteristics of the process of changing the world through work can be contrasted with the phenomenon of experimentation. Experimentation which involves merely the manipulation of some of the existing elements in a social order in an attempt to discover various alternate forms the order may take is not yet revolutionary praxis. It is a rationalization of what is given.

An experiment can be value free if one proceeds so as not to disturb the world. Work can never be value free and must always interfere with the world and change it. An experiment is practical because it helps us to see in a particular case how the existing order can best be adapted to changing circumstances. Praxis disturbs the world, upsets the world, changes the world, revolutionizes the world. Praxis and work are social phenomena which require changes in the social order. Work is not merely a technical ordering of what is given. It involves the creation of a new order—a new order which can be created only by a democratic movement. Through revolutionary praxis a new world is created which is qualitatively different from the old order. An experiment which merely orders what is given does not go beyond what is present. The results of an experiment can only be applied to improve the operation of the existing social order; the results of revolutionary praxis are contained in the very process of creating a new world in which to work.

To take just one example of liberal experimentation and its inability to introduce a radical change in the existing society, let us look at the health care situation in the United States.

An Example of Authentic Marxism

In all major universities of the United States, the medical schools and research centers require the greatest funds and staff. Tremendous amounts of money and a large number of experiments have shown what to do to a particular person, or even to particular groups, in order to solve certain health problems. From the application of money and experiments, we now know what needs to be done in particular instances to give good health care so that individuals can be rehabilitated into society.

At the same time, in cases where individuals do not need to be treated to fit into society, but the social order itself needs to be changed, the United States, because of its dominant liberal theory and economic system, is helpless in both conducting research and instituting genuine reforms. For example, the infant mortality rate in the United States is higher than in many other industrialized countries. Still, it is not recognized that in order to reduce this rate, it is necessary to introduce a radical change in the way of living for a substantial part of the population. To bring about this change requires not an experiment, but work; it requires a fundamental change in the economic and social order producing the high infant mortality rate.

One could give other examples of cases where knowledge gained through experimentation is available but cannot be used because of the social system which is present. There is evidence that the individual housing patterns produced by the capitalistic order are both socially and architecturally unsound for society as a whole. We know that the blacks in America live in a state of bondage hardly better than slavery. We know that the educational system in America treats men as machines when they need to be humanized. To solve these problems we do not need more experiments as much as we need more work which changes the world. The problem today is not so much to have knowledge about the world, but to create a new kind of world. In almost all areas of life it has become clear that praxis is needed—a praxis which goes beyond experimentation. The authentic Marxist tradition is a tradition of praxis. It understands that social changes are brought about by a revolutionary movement of people working to create a social and democratic order in which genuine praxis is possible.

The theoretical failure of Stalinism which crippled the democratic Marxist tradition was the failure to distinguish between purely tactical considerations—practical considerations, which may be more or less correct at a given moment—and the theoretical development of Marxism. As Lukacs puts it,

> In other words: instead of following the true method of Marxism and developing a strategy and tactics from an analysis of the events, tactical decisions—right or wrong decisions—were decisive, and a theory was built on these.[18]

Both Stalinism and liberal democracy have been dominated by a crude pragmatism in which the "practical" action is praised and encouraged. Theory was motivated by tactical considerations rather than thought being rooted in theoretical discussion.

The new democrats who are a part of the revolutionary Marxist tradition appear to be impractical, because they call into question not only particular appearances of the contemporary order, but also the way of life and the social and economic institutions which exist. But they understand that good political praxis can emerge only out of an analysis of the forces present in the existing order. This analysis and understanding of society cannot be replaced by short-range practical decisions within the current order. Loyalty to the revolutionary movement is the chief characteristic of the authentic Marxist. A new democratic theory which is a development out of and beyond liberal democracy and Stalinism is in the early stage of development. Although the new democratic theory will be developed only on the basis of praxis, the direction in which the theory is beginning to develop is becoming clearer. In the following chapters we shall turn to some of the specific problems the new democratic theory attempts to face and to the possibilities present for the development of a genuinely revolutionary theory and movement.

References

ACZEL, TAMAS, and MERAY, TIBOR, *The Revolt of the Mind. A Case History of Intellectual Resistance Behind the Iron Curtain*, Praeger, New York, 1959.

> A personal account of the role played by writers and intellectuals in preparing the way for the 1956 uprising. Despite the fact that the authors are clearly anticommunist, Lukacs is portrayed as a man with one primary concern—his loyalty to the revolutionary movement. An accurate account of Lukacs's role in 1956 is yet to be written, but this book does provide a warm and enthusiastic character sketch of Lukacs during that time.

CARY, WILLIAM, *New Man or No Man*, New Bearings, Bolton, Mass., 1969.

> A sympathetic treatment of changes underway in Central Europe. One chapter deals with a conversation with Lukacs. The whole book is weak theoretically, but it does show in what sense positive changes are underway in the Marxist tradition.

GOLDMANN, LUCIEN, *The Human Sciences and Philosophy*, Grossman Publishers, Cape Editions, London, 1969.

> An early (1952) study by a Marxist who was heavily influenced by Lukacs's *History and Class Consciousness*.

GRAMSCI, ANTONIO, *The Modern Prince and Other Writings*, International Publishers, New York, 1957.

> Gramsci is one of the most important Marxists. This collection is the first publication of his works in English. Judging from the interest shown in his works now, he will become increasingly important in a revival of Marxism. Gramsci, an Italian, died in 1937 after eleven years of imprisonment in fascist Italy.

An Example of Authentic Marxism

KORSCH, KARL, *Karl Marx*, Wiley, New York, 1938.
> The only book in English by the German Korsch. His most important work, for the purposes of our discussion here, was his book *Marxismus und Philosophie* (Marxism and Philosophy), second edition, 1930. Korsch, Gramsci, and Lukacs are being widely discussed in the movement in Europe, although their influence has been minimal in the United States.

LITCHTHEIM, GEORGE, "Lukacs, György," *International Encyclopedia of Social Sciences*, vol. 9, pp. 488–491, Macmillian, New York, 1968.
> Lichtheim treats the development of Lukacs up to 1953 and dismisses the work of Lukacs since then, but he does give a short introduction to the life and works of Lukacs.

MEGILL, KENNETH, "Georg Lukacs As an Ontologist," *Studies in Soviet Thought*, vol. IX, no. 4, December, 1969, pp. 334–353.
> A more technical discussion of the latest development of Lukacs than that included in this chapter.

WATNICK, MORRIS, "Relativism and Class Consciousness: Georg Lukacs," in *Revisionism*, edited by Leopold Labedz, Praeger, New York, 1962.
> An adequate introduction to Lukacs and some of his earlier writings and controversies. It is unfortunate that the essay is included in a book with this title.

ZITTA, VICTOR, *Georg Lukacs' Marxism. Alienation, Dialectics, Revolution*, Martinus Nijhoff, The Hague, 1964.
> Unfortunately this is the only book in English on Lukacs. Zitta's failure to understand even the barest outlines of Lukacs's philosophy and his desperate anticommunism make the entire work less than useful.

5
The Democratic
Coalition

*The proper application of the term "democracy" is to a
constitution in which the free-born and poor control the
government.*
ARISTOTLE

Democracy today, as always, means a rule by the people, that is,
a social order which is controlled by those who live and work in
society. Yet a general discussion of democracy easily becomes
romantic and irrelevant unless it is related to existing social
movements and social phenomena. A correct democratic theory
is based on the experience of a democratic movement and is
expressed in terms of how men relate to their work.

In the West and in the East a new democratic theory is now
emerging from the parallel experiences of opposition to the
political order established by the United States and the Soviet
Union. In the West, both black and white radicals are being
created, while in the East, the tradition of democratic Marxism
is being rediscovered. The development of the new democratic
theory is based on this democratic movement and a new coalition
which can serve as a carrier of fundamental social change. The

failure of liberal democracy (with its emphasis on representation) and of dialectical materialism (with its emphasis on the authority of a bureaucratic party) is a reflection of the collapse of the democratic coalition of the nineteenth and twentieth centuries. If democracy is to be more than a utopian notion, a new democratic coalition must be forged out of forces which are a part of the effective reality of the twentieth century.

In Aristotle's *Politics*, and earlier in Plato's *Republic*, the two first great political philosophers described the process by which the poor gain control of the political institutions. Their descriptions of the mechanism through which the poor and the masses can seize control has been relevant for democratic movements throughout history and is still relevant today. The new democrats are a part of this revolutionary democratic tradition, but their theory is not simply one more addition to the democratic theories which have been put forward since the great Greek philosophers. For Aristotle and Plato, the democratic social order was one passing stage among many; for the new democrats, democracy is a necessary social order in the twentieth century.

Three main groups have traditionally formed a coalition to work for democracy:

1. The poor.

2. Those left outside the political and social institutions.

3. Those who have an interest, either personally or because they understand the nature of historical development, in a democratic order.

If we examine the traditional democratic coalition of the nineteenth and early twentieth century—the coalition which supported liberal democracy and dialectical materialism— and understand why it is no longer adequate, then we can better analyze the new democratic coalition which is now in the process of forming.

The poor have always been a source of trouble in a well-ordered society. They do not work as those in positions of domination expect them to work, and, above all, they seem to have little stake in the preservation of order and "good sense." They have traditionally been a substantial part of the population, and their support has been necessary for a revolutionary movement. The poor have little to lose if a drastic and fundamental social change takes place. On one hand, they are the hopeless members of society; on the other hand, they are the hope for all those looking for a way to change society. At least formally, the eradication of poverty has been an important part of the program of both the liberal democrats and the dialectical materialists. In the developed countries of the world, the poor are no longer in the majority, but the continued presence of a large number of poor people has only highlighted the failure of the traditional democratic theories to wipe out poverty completely. The liberal democrats are faced with constant problems of creating a workable program to raise the standard of those living in poverty. In the bastion of the liberal democratic countries, the United States, the poor (according to the definition of those in power) still make up 20 per cent of the population, and there seems to be no effective way within the current order to completely eliminate poverty. The existence of poverty is incompatible with the liberal democratic ideology. Yet in liberal democratic societies it does not seem possible to eradicate this condition. Though the number of poor has been reduced, they remain one of the potentially revolutionary democratic forces in our society today.

But the poor alone have never been able to seize power and sustain a revolutionary movement. At critical times they are

The Democratic Coalition

essential for a mass movement, but other groups must join with them in order for the revolutionary movement to be successful. In previous democratic coalitions there have been various classes and groups which were denied full participation in the political system and which were deprived in a social and cultural sense. These groups demanded changes in society to enable them to develop their own capacities more fully. The poor have been and are the natural allies of groups and classes which demand greater political and social power.

In the course of social and economic change new classes have arisen to demand democratization. For example, when the great feudal systems began to break up in Europe, the primary democratic force was composed of the new capitalists, who demanded participation in the political and social institutions. That is, when the old political institutions were no longer adequate to represent the people who had gained economic and social power, they joined with others to promote a democratization of society. The capitalist forces were initially revolutionary and demanded a broadening of the base of government. The American and French revolutions, together with the success of the reform movement in England in the early part of the nineteenth century, which resulted in repeal of the Corn Laws and broadening of suffrage, marked the conquest of the liberal democratic forces in most of Europe and America. The democratization which came with the growth of the capitalist system wiped out the feudal structures which had dominated society for centuries. The small and large businessmen demanded participation in government and society on an equal basis. Merit (understood as the ability to accumulate property), not family position, was to be the criterion for social position and advancement. In order to impose this order, centuries of revolutionary wars were fought to broaden suffrage

68

and wipe out traditional privileges. Power was transferred to a class which had grown up as the capitalist economic system developed. The liberal democratic theory served as the theoretical expression of this revolutionary force. The government was seen to be a protector of property and individual rights, while decisions were to be made by the majority of the free property-owning citizens. For centuries this theory was revolutionary, and those who would benefit from a liberal democratic political and social order fought many battles before they were successful.

As the capitalist system progressed, a new class was in turn created which demanded democratization. The capitalist economic system, in order to function efficiently, requires large industries staffed by workers who have no productive property but their labor. The massive migration from the land to the city and the complete destruction of the guild system created a large class of workers who were dependent upon the capitalist system for their livelihood. These workers served as part of the democratic coalition which demanded that the government ensure every citizen a minimum of economic security. The trade unions and the socialist parties became a new revolutionary force and in various countries, in various ways, sought to capture control of the governmental machinery. The workers were often poor or formed a natural alliance with the poor; but one must clearly distinguish between the kind of worker who seeks an end to the fear of unemployment and still hopes to advance within the system through education or hard work, and the poor, who are left outside the productive system.

The poor and the workers provided the basis for almost all democratic movements in the nineteenth and twentieth centuries. In Russia the classical coalition of workers and peasants was first formed in an open and revolutionary manner.

In 1917 power was seized, and a socialist government was established. In the United States, fifteen years later, Franklin Roosevelt formed a coalition of the poor (both white and black) and the workers (trade unions), which served as the basis for the uninterrupted power of the Democratic Party for a generation. In England the Labour Party replaced the Liberal Party as the second major political party and periodically governed in the interests of the poor and the workers. Throughout Europe social democratic parties, with more or less success, sought to seize power on the strength of the workers and the poor. The democratic forces were based upon these two groups which had been created by the capitalist system, but whose demands could not be met within the system.

In all democratic movements a third group has formed a part of the democratic coalition. Often this group is composed of the intellectuals who see and feel the fact that large portions of the population are powerless. In the eighteenth and nineteenth centuries there were numerous examples of intellectuals who aligned themselves with the democratic forces, not because they themselves were poor or excluded from the political and social institutions, but because they came to understand how a better life was possible for the masses. The intellectuals, whether we think of Rousseau, John Stuart Mill, Marx, or Lenin, have played an important role in bringing consciousness to the democratic movement. It would be unwise, however, to conclude that all intellectuals, simply because they are intellectuals, have an interest in democratization. On the contrary, the vast majority of intellectuals serve as apologists for the dominant political and social forces and put their talents at the service of the ruling forces. Nevertheless some intellectuals, partly because they have always occupied a special role in society, have had a sense of freedom and perspective, which allowed them to participate in a democratic movement.

Until World War II the classical democratic coalition, in almost all parts of the world, was composed of the poor, the workers, and some intellectuals. In varying combinations, depending upon the situation, this coalition successfully defended and instituted the liberal democratic and dialectical materialistic theories and social systems. But more recently it appears that the old coalition has collapsed, just as the old theories have collapsed. Revolution seems to be out of date. The workers have fought and won many battles, both in the East and in the West. In many countries full employment is guaranteed by union protection or state policy. The levels of living have constantly risen. The class structure, so it is said, does display a considerable amount of flexibility. The workers can send their children to school and can hope that hard work will enable them to become part of a higher class.

The success of the workers in winning their immediate demands has also reduced the number of poor. Poverty, on the massive scale which once existed, has been eased. Many people still live in poverty, but they tend more and more to be the old, the handicapped, and (in the United States) those who have been systematically discriminated against because of their skin color. The poor are still there, but they are no longer an organized group which seeks political power, except for the blacks in the United States.

Finally, the intellectuals, particularly since World War II, have found personal advancement within the existing order to be more to their advantage than any principled opposition to the system. In the continuing search for security, each intellectual hopes that one more publication will bring him the authority and freedom for which he longs. In the socialist countries, education has been tremendously encouraged, and those who have succeeded in the educational system have been rewarded with better-paying jobs and the possibilities for security and a sense of power. The chance for personal advancement has left the vast majority of intellectuals with little desire for a fundamental change in the economic and social system.

Thus the members of the old democratic coalition—the poor, the workers, and some intellectuals—all, we are told, seem to have an interest in defending the current system and are opposed to any revolutionary democratic movement. Those who fought for specific economic and social goals appear to have been successful, and in the process they have ceased to be revolutionary.

If the new democratic theory is to be meaningful, a democratic coalition must be formed, not just in one country, but throughout the world. Only if a coalition interested in fundamental change can be constructed, can the new democratic theory be more than the wishful thinking of dissatisfied minorities. Although it would indeed be mere illusion to imagine the poor, the workers, and the intellectuals as revolutionary forces in the form in which they are now organized, there is good reason to believe that the potential for a democratic coalition may not be dead. Although the workers have often won some of the immediate goals for which they fought—higher wages and job security—they have not gained long-range control over their working situation. Their demands have been met, not by giving the workers political and social power, but by providing a sense of well-being within the present system. Such a "solution" can only be temporary, at least on a wide scale, since there will continue to be problems which can be solved only if the workers can gain control over their working situation. Above all, the *quality* of the work done by the worker cannot be substantially improved until he can begin to exercise real control over his working situation. Today the worker can only hope that the work week will be shortened so that he may live another life in his free time. But as we shall see later, free time is no longer free. It is manipulated and dominated by those in power. The shortening of the work day has not removed the causes of alienation which made the worker a part of the revolutionary movement; it has merely broadened and extended alienation to free time as well as working time. The revolutionary potential of the working people is still there, even though their organizations and the whole force of society push them toward cooperation with the existing order. This cooperation is maintained by giving hope that there will be both more free time and higher wages and also that the workers, or their children, will be able to escape from the working class. But the hope for individual escape does not satisfy the primary democratic demand that the worker have control over his working situation. Until this demand can be met, there is still a revolutionary potential in the working class.

The intellectuals have also found a kind of satisfaction in the current system. They believe that they can think freely. They hope for individual advancement within the existing order. They can, however, neither control their own working situation, nor can they exericise control in society as a whole. These goals can be realized only if they join with others to gain real power, not just as individuals, but as members of a democratic movement.

The diffusion of the traditional democratic coalition has been accomplished, not by meeting the demands of these groups, but by offering individuals the hope for a better life and security within the current order. For a democratic revolutionary movement, it would be foolish to look to the organizations which claim to represent the traditional coalition today; it would be equally foolish to deny that the revolutionary potential exists. A correct democratic theory must succeed in showing that the demands of the old coalition were only apparently met. There is still an interest in a democratization in which people can gain control over the institutions in which they work and live.

The new coalition, like other democratic coalitions, will be built out of three major groups: the poor, those who are outside the political and social institutions, and those who support a democratic movement because they see the possibility for a new democratic order. But the new coalition cannot be merely a reassembly of the democratic movement which existed in the early part of this century; a new analysis is needed of the social forces which promote a democratic order in the world today.

Although the major industrial nations have reduced the number of poor in their own societies, they have not eliminated poverty on a global basis. When the world as a whole is considered, the number of poor has increased substantially since World War II. With the success of the struggle against the colonial powers, new forces have been brought into political life. In the nineteenth century and the early part of this century, the democratic movement was almost entirely a movement within the major industrial, imperialist nations. Their colonies were still involved in the struggle for national independence. Now, however, the poor nations are a new political force. Their political life can no longer be dictated by the wealthy nations. As the poor nations begin to hope and struggle for a better way of life, a decisive new force of poor people is born, a force which has an interest in a democratic political and social order. The poor nations have become a political force with an interest in revolutionary change.

The struggle of the blacks in the United States is a part of the worldwide struggle of the poor to achieve a democratic order. More and more the blacks in the United States have understood that they are brothers and sisters of the poor and oppressed of the world, because of their common relationship as subjects of oppression by the wealthy. The poor are uniting as a revolutionary democratic force. They have one basic demand: to remove domination and oppression by the wealthy. This demand can be fully met only if a democratic social and political order can be created. In a new and radical way the poor have not only the potential for participation in the democratic movement, but also the ability to build a movement which is already beginning to have great force in the world. If they are to succeed in their struggle against those who control their lives, they must take part in a genuinely international democratic movement together with other forces seeking a democratic order.

Among the so-called middle class in the industrialized countries a new kind of poverty—cultural poverty—is beginning to be perceived. The search after material comfort has run into a dead end. An increasing number of young people are seeing that the lives lived by their parents, who claim to be successful within the system, are poor and that a life of quality has not been created in spite of the apparent material abundance. The culturally deprived today are not only those who live in material poverty, but also those who are isolated and enslaved in much more subtle ways. The perception of their own poverty in the midst of plenty has been one of the crucial experiences for many of these joining the new democratic coalition.

Within recent years the particular oppression of women, both inside and outside the movement, has been recognized, and the struggle for women's liberation has become an important part of the struggle against the existing society. The liberation of women will require both an end to their particular exploitation in the working situation and a transformation of their relationship to men in the family.

In the industrialized nations of the world the working class, in a traditional sense, is shrinking, both in numbers and in importance in the productive process. A new kind of worker is being created who must be educated and who has to be capable of understanding the productive process in which he takes part. These new workers must be educated to be creative, but in the working situation they are expected to be docile and to be in a dependency relationship similar to that of the traditional working class. New groups of educated people are treated as workers and have less and less interest in preserving the current economic and social order. Among these new educated groups are engineers, teachers (who are already more numerous than farmers in the United States), nurses, technicians, and skilled workers in the service industries. They have only begun to recognize that their interests no longer lie with the ruling forces of society, but with those seeking a change in the social and economic system. Of course, it remains to be seen whether the professional organizations will be more radical than the trade unions are now. At the present time only a few organizations of professionals are militant, and it would appear that they must all become more radical, given their goal of participation in the control of their working situation.

A characteristic of the new members of the working class is that the distinction between intellectuals and workers has become more and more blurred. The universities in both East and West have already become institutions designed to train people who will become part of the working class. Education has become a mass product and a university education a necessity for many workers. No longer is the university the preserve of the aristocrats and managers of the social system. The educational program at universities everywhere in the world is aimed not at producing gentlemen and leaders of society, but at producing the new kind of worker who is essential for a materially productive society. The students and intellectuals, both where they learn and where they work, are treated as workers. Like other workers the students, who are trained as intellectual technicans, have little objective interest in the preservation of the current order. In fact increasing numbers of the brighter students are discovering they have no subjective interest in its preservation either. In this situation they find their allies among the few teachers in the university who recognize that they are treated as workers and who share the desire for democratization.

The products of the universities are workers because they have nothing but their labor time to sell. These workers, of course, are given the exterior trappings of professionals, who are a part of the ruling class, but in their working situation they have more in common with the traditonal workers than with the administrators of the ruling class interests.

The new democratic movement and theory are a product of these three new forces which have recently developed: the poor, as an international force; the technical and service workers who are educated; and the young intellectuals—students and teachers. The possibility for building a new democratic movement is there. There are signs that the revolt against the post world war order has been led by these groups, who have an interest in a democratic order and in a fundamental social and political change. In addition, those struggling for liberation from particular forms of oppression, especially the blacks and women, will play a leading role in the movement to bring about a revolutionary transformation of society. The democratic coalition will develop as these new groupings perceive their common interest with those who were traditionally part of the democratic coalition, such as the unskilled and skilled workers.

The new democratic coalition has already formed in various ways with varying degrees of success in many countries of the world. It will be successful in achieving control of political and social development only if it can align itself with those in the traditional coalition whose demands have not been fully met. In the course of revolutions and rebellions, which have become widespread, the coalition involving the poor, the workers, and some young intellectuals has assumed various forms. The new democratic coalition has a definite chance of success in establishing a democratic order in which men can control their own affairs. In a modern industrial society those interested in a democratic order make up the vast majority of the population. As we shall see later, the most efficient and humane social order can be produced if the new coalition is successful.

In all previous democratic coalitions it was necessary to establish a new kind of subordination in society. The democracy of the Greeks was based on a large class of slaves, who provided the material and economic goods so that a cultivated and meaningful life for the ruling class could be achieved. During feudalism a large class of serfs was necessary to ensure that the productive forces could be maintained and developed. Capitalism required workers who could be utilized to produce, but who were not capable of governing their own affairs.

Now, for a society to function well, the destruction of the system of subordination has become necessary. Such a destruction opens the possibility for creating a democratic order which can be stable. The new democratic forces are not dependent upon a government which can protect their property, for they

References

are without property in the classical sense. Instead they require a government which can protect the working conditions and ensure that man's creativity as a worker can be maintained. Such a government can only be democratic. Such a government is possible today in a new and radical sense.

References

FERMAN, LOUIS A., KORNBLUH, JOYCE L., and HABER, ALAN, *Poverty in America*, University of Michigan Press, Ann Arbor, 1965.
> A collection of articles showing how widespread poverty is in America and the kind of life lived by the poor. Written during the early days of the poverty program, it makes no real attempt at a radical analysis of the failure of the system to solve its problems.

GORZ, ANDRE, *Strategy for Labor. A Radical Proposal*, Beacon Press, Boston, 1967.
> Gorz gives convincing arguments that the workers have an interest in fundamental social change, and he offers alternatives for a movement in advanced capitalist countries. One of the most important and provocative books on the strategy of the democratic radical movement.

HAMILTON, RICHARD F., *Affluence and the French Worker in the Fourth Republic*, Princeton University Press, Princeton, N.J., 1967.
> An empirical study of the politics of the French worker, which indicates that rising affluence does not necessarily mean a de-radicalization of the working class.

HARRINGTON, MICHAEL, *Toward a Democratic Left: A Radical Program for a New Majority*, Pelican, Baltimore, 1968.
> A social democratic view of how a new democratic coalition may be possible.

LEGGETT, JOHN C., *Class, Race, and Labor. Working-Class Consciousness in Detroit*, Oxford University Press, New York, 1968.
> An extremely valuable study of the working class in Detroit, which shows, by using the techniques developed by social sciences, that working class consciousness still exists. An epilogue discusses the

79

possibility for the working class consciousness to be turned into revolutionary class consciousness and the necessity for the elimination of racism for the working class to achieve its goals.

MILLER, S. M., and RIESSMAN, FRANK, *Social Class and Social Policy*, Basic Books, New York, 1968.

> Based on a program of "radical reform rather than revolution" (p. 282), there is an attempt to formulate the positive elements in the culture of the poor and the workers. The final conclusions lead to a supporting of the integration process, but there is some interesting information given along the way that could be used for a revolutionary position.

SHOSTAK, ARTHUR B., and GOMBERG, WILLIAM, *Blue-Collar World. Studies of the American Worker*, Prentice-Hall, Englewood Cliffs, N.I., 1964.

> A collection of sociological studies of the American worker, which contains valuable information and at least attempts to overcome the middle-class bias of most sociological studies. Although it is difficult to conclude much from such a large number of studies, it is clear that little is really known about the kind of life of the worker and the possibility for liberation on his terms, rather than on terms imposed from outside. Of particular interest are several articles which deal with the relationship of the worker and the poor.

6
The New Political Language

> *It is above all necessary to avoid postulating "society" once again as an abstraction confronting the individual. The individual is the social being. . . . Though man is a unique individual—and it is just his particularity which makes him an individual, a really individual communal being—he is equally the whole, the ideal whole, the subjective existence of society as thought and experienced.*
> MARX

Our argument has taken us from a discussion of the failure of the traditional democratic theories, dialectical materialism and liberal democracy, to a consideration of the possible constituents of a new democratic movement. In this chapter we shall examine the new language being developed by the movement to describe social and political life and some of the reasons why traditional political language has been discredited. The development of this new political language clearly indicates the presence of a new democratic theory.

Whitehead has said that philosophical theories are seldom refuted; they just become uninteresting and are ignored. The new democratic theory does not, in any direct sense, refute the traditional democratic theories, but instead looks upon the

81

liberal democratic theory and dialectical materialism as being wooden and dull attempts to describe contemporary reality. In earlier chapters the language of the dominant democratic theories has hardly been used. The usual discussions of all the terms traditionally used—majority rule and minority rights, the relationship of the individual and society, and the place of the nation state in world affairs—were missing. The new democrats are developing a language which is more adequate to discuss political affairs. Using a new language does not *solve* any problems, but it does permit us to look upon social reality in a radically new way.

The traditional terms are abstractions from the social reality in which we live. Nowhere do we find any societies or working situations to which these terms could be concretely applied. The abstractions used in the formulation of the traditional democratic theories are not adequate in defining present social reality. The best the liberal democrats or dialectical materialists can do is to reason in self-affirming fashion. They accept a given nation or society as democratic by definition (for example, the United States or the Soviet Union) and proceed to define democracy by describing the decision-making procedures in the nation or group which is already assumed to be democratic. Such a way of arguing can be used only to defend the status quo by giving a name to systems which do not deserve it. A new language which can describe the world in which men actually live and work needs to be articulated if a genuinely new democratic theory is to be developed.

Individuals and Society

In much of current democratic theory it is assumed that there are only two kinds of entities: individuals and societies. We can study individuals in psychology, and societies in sociology and anthropology. If we begin to examine any particular concrete situation, it is impossible to determine when the individual is acting socially and when society is working through individuals. Countless philosophical and practical problems have been generated in political discussions by using units called individuals and units called societies.

The problem of the nature of individuals and societies is really an instance of the traditional philosophical problem of particulars and universals. Almost all major traditions of twentieth-century philosophy have come to agree that it is a mistake to view the world as if it were composed of either individuals or one large unit. Instead, modern philosophers prefer to speak of family definitions of terms, in which we specify the meaning of a word by giving various examples of its uss in ordinary language. As Wittgenstein, along with many other philosophers, put it, "The meaning of a word is its use." We use the word "individual" in many different ways. By using general terms we cannot specify the *nature* of the individual. Whitehead called the tendency to look upon objects as if they had one particular location the "fallacy of simple location." The assumption that individuals are units which build societies is the political expression of the fallacy of simple location.

It is not surprising that the new democrats do not accept the traditional notions of the individual and society, since any complicated working process today cannot be done by an isolated individual. The working process which takes place in a highly industrialized society is a social process. It is cooperative; that is, the individual can work only together with other individuals. Society can best be viewed as a result of the cooperation of individuals who are united on the basis of a common working situation. In *Capital* Marx described how the process of cooperation was required for the construction of an industrial society. The cooperation which he described has been extended to more and more areas of life today, and an efficient industrial system must be cooperative in the working situation.

The traditional liberal theory, from Locke onward, has assumed that thè worker is an individual who interacts immediately with nature to acquire property. According to this view, society is created by the agreement of free individuals to protect their property. Although this description was applicable to a limited degree in an early phase of capitalism, it is difficult to find anyone who works in this sense today. Instead, nearly all working and living situations are highly socialized. The dialectical materialists, on the other hand, have done no better theoretically than the liberals, since they have conceived work to be totally socialized. They have correctly understood that work in an industrial society must be social, but they have forgotten the equal importance of individuality in the working process.

Because the working process is necessarily social, a social theory fails if it rests upon either the assumption that there are individuals who are particular entities which create society, or if it claims that there are no individuals at all, but merely socially determined beings. We commit what Whitehead calls the "fallacy of simple location" when we assume either that society is an artificial entity or that individuals are merely products of society. The liberal democrats have tended to commit the former fallacy; the dialectical materialists have committed the latter. Both theories make the same fundamental mistake of seeing individuals and society as the fundamental units of social organization.

It may sometimes be *useful* to speak of individuals; it may even be *justifiable* if we bear in mind that we are using an abstraction. We can correctly speak of individual rights, of individuals expressing their will at the polls, of individuals participating in the process of working. We can conduct investigations of the way in which individuals act, and we can look upon literature, for example, as a means of describing reality, in which the special characteristics of man are developed. The individual does have integrity, for he loves, hates, dies, suffers, rejoices, and thinks. Any political theory (such as dialectical materialism) which suppresses the individual is bound to fail. But in all our discussions of individuals we must bear in mind that the individual is in society and that any discussion of the individual must be an abstraction from the concrete social reality in which he lives and works. The nonsocial individual of the liberal society has no concrete existence.

Similarly, it is possible to speak a language of society, just as we can speak a language of the individual. We can show how man is socially determined, how the forms of life and the customs and habits he has are determined by the nature of the society in which he lives. It is sometimes good and useful to speak this language, but we must be aware that to speak of society apart from the individual is an abstraction and is not a description of the real life which we live. If *society* and *individual* are understood as various perspectives on the life we lead, then we can see that it is indeed useful to have a science of society and a science of the individual. To claim that science completely exhausts the description of reality would, of course, be incorrect, since no description can completely capture the specialness of human forms of association.

Integration and Specialness

The new democrats have begun to develop an alternative language to describe the social and political reality of the twentieth century by focusing on the specialness of groups in community. The more or less unconscious rejection of the terms individual and society have not, however, been understood in connection with the rejection in contemporary philosophy of both the monistic (society is the only real entity) and pluralistic (individuals are the only real entities) positions. It is necessary to develop a new kind of language to describe the place of the individual in the new democratic theory.

When the new democrats refuse to use the traditional language of individual and society or refuse to speak at great length about the relationship of the individual and society, they are in their own practical way· accepting the fact that another language must be found to describe and discuss social reality, a new language which does not commit us to a language of individualism or a language of collectivism. For this reason, the new democrats use terms such as *community* or *cooperatives* or *workers' democracies*—all of which attempt to express the concrete way in which men are associated as individuals in society.

The use of the language of the individual and society assumes that there is some basic conflict between individuals and the society in which they live. The problem, if this is true, is to integrate people into the society or to create a society in which integration is possible. Instead of seeing a democratic order as one in which people and communities are encouraged to develop their own special interests and needs, there is a constant pressure to bring all groups within the consensus. The new democrats, whether they formulate their program in terms of Black Power or in terms of the democratic Marxist tradition, place their emphasis on the specialness of man. A black man is not an individual, in an isolated sense, but is a special person because he is black. A worker in society is not only a member of society, but is a special person with special skills, needs, and potentialities.

To speak of man as being special denies neither his individuality nor the fact that he is a social being. The special is a radically different kind of category, which mediates between the individual object and the general. (This fact was first seen by Hegel in his *Logic* and developed by Lukacs in his *Aesthetics*.) When the radicals in the United States reject the traditional "individualism" in the liberal democratic theory, they are arguing for the recognition of the specialness of human persons and human communities. Similarly, the Marxists, who are rebeling against the over-centralization of society, are asking that the specialness of various working situations and communities be recognized and developed.

By focusing on individuals and societies as special entities, with their own careers and their own needs, we can provide a criterion for judging the extent to which a democratic society is present. A democratic society is one which encourages and develops the specialness of people and communities and does not integrate the individual into society. It must be emphasized that to be special, one need not be peculiar. Pecularity is a kind of individuality which sets one off from others. To be special is to affirm one's place as a member of a community. By emphasizing the specialness of man and communities the new democrats have begun to develop a language which more adequately describes social reality, and a language which is proper for a better understanding of the democratic way of life.

Majority Rule

Without a doubt, the principle of majority rule was at the heart of the democratic program of the nineteenth and early twentieth centuries. All democrats, whether they were liberals, socialists, or communists, have been united in the demand for universal suffrage. The demand for majority rule was important when large masses of the population were simply excluded from all political life. Even Marx and Engels, to the ends of their lives, saw socialism to be the true democracy *because* the proletariat composed the majority in most West European countries. To succeed in getting universal suffrage would bring, so it was thought, democracy. Once the proletariat, as the great majority, was allowed to express its will, then democracy would begin to be a reality.

The fact that majority rule has always been thought to be an important part of democratic theory does not mean that it has ever been possible for the majority to rule in the way called for by the theory. At best, the principle of majority rule works only at the level where individuals making decisions are aware of available alternatives. At best, majority rule is no more than a convenient way to settle the opinion of the community; it is not the essential characteristic of democracy or rule by the people. In a small group majority rule does not mean that opinions and decisions are arrived at by voting procedures, but rather that mutal interests exist and that within a community it is possible to arrive at decisions which are binding on all. In other words, the existence of a community of interest is more important than the actual voting process itself.

Rousseau saw that the state of the community is more important than the individual expression of will and distinguished between what he called the "will of all" and the "general will." He argued that it is possible to achieve very different results, depending upon how the will of various citizens is counted and which particular interests are allowed to form the will of the individuals. It has become increasingly clear that it is a serious mistake to confuse the will expressed by the individuals in society with the general will of the people. Particularly in advanced industrial societies it is possible to create and manipulate the will of individuals in society and thus control the majority. In this process the principle of majority rule often functions to inhibit, rather than to free, man. Much of traditional democratic theory has mistakenly held that if we could get everyone's individual will taken into account, then it would be possible to assume that the general will of the community is adequately expressed.

Since the principle of majority rule has been abstracted from the situation where a community of interest exists and real discussion takes place, it has ceased to play the important role which was established for it in the traditional democratic theory. In fact, as an abstract principle, majority rule does not seem to be essential for democracy. Rather, what is essential is that the crucial decisions which are made in a social situation are controlled by the members who actually live and work in that organization. The principle of majority rule can have nothing at all to do with democracy and can even serve as a cover for a decision-making process which is undemocratic. In both the East and West elections are regularly held in which it is claimed that the majority decides the crucial issues of the country. It has become clear that these elections—whether they are held in the United States or in a communist country—have little to do with determining the course which society will take.

It is being realized today that the essential feature of democracy is that the members of the community *control* their communal life and are able to exercise *self-control* over their own fate. While this control and self-control may be expressed in a system where majority rule is present, majority rule is not a necessary condition for their expression. There are alternate ways of arriving at decisions in a democracy. Majority rule is only one of them. Control and self-control are concepts which more adequately describe free decisions made both in our individual life and in our social life. The language which speaks of "wills" that are computed into majorities and minorities manifests itself in a tortuous and unreal description of any actual decision procedure. It will lead those who understand the impossibility of majority rule in most significant areas of life to conclude that democracy is only an impossible ideal. Majority rule is seen, by the new democrats, in its proper light, as a useful mechanism instead of being democracy itself.

Minority Rights

A corollary of the principle of majority rule has been that there are certain rights which the minority retains, regardless of how the majority might decide any particular issue. The rights of man are said to be fundamental, unassailable rights of the individual, which are given to him by his creator or which he has by nature. Among the rights of man which are commonly listed are freedom of speech, freedom of assembly, and freedom of religion. As stated in the most recent attempt at outlining them—the Universal Declaration of Human Rights, drafted by the United Nations—man's rights are quite different from what they were thought to be in the eighteenth century. Among the more modern rights of man are included the right to employment, the right to an education, and the right of women to full equality with men. It is clear that rights have a history and that what today are taken to be the rights of man were not always thought to be so.

Similarly, certain rights which were assumed two hundred years ago, such as the natural right of property, are not now universally held to be rights of man. In an early draft of the Declaration of Independence the phrase "life, liberty, and the pursuite of happiness" read "life, liberty and property." In most countries with some form of socialism, it has been recognized that no one has an inalienable right to property. Even in the United States it has been generally accepted that no one has the right to deny access to his property solely on the basis of race, which means that the right to property is not a "natural" right, but one that exists only within a social context.

The doctrine of natural rights was originally a revolutionary principle which was urged by those who were seeking a fundamental change in the nature of society. Today, however, the doctrine of natural rights is generally used to protect the present power structure. Thus we say that we have freedom of the press, meaning that anyone who has sufficient capital and is willing and able to attract sufficient advertising is free to operate a newspaper. As a matter of fact, the distribution of news has been taken over by large enterprises, which can exist only as long as they do not offend the basic economic and social structure. We say that we have the right to free assembly, but we find that the buildings are controlled by the institutions which control the economic and social life of the country. We find, repeatedly, that the language of natural rights and minority rights is used to protect those who are already in a position of power and influence. It is seldom used to protect those who advocate a fundamental change in society. Natural rights and minority rights have been turned from principles protecting the right of revolution into principles which perpetuate the status quo.

The problem with the language of natural rights is not that there are no natural rights which need to be protected, but rather that natural rights, when they are interpreted abstractly, serve to shut off avenues for changing society. In some respects, the new democrats argue more forcefully than anyone else in favor of the rights of the minority. Particularly in the East European countries the struggle for democracy is very often still the struggle to gain the right to conduct research freely, to organize freely, and to publish freely. Perhaps the best way to understand the role which natural rights play in any democratic society is that they are a necessary, but not a sufficient, condition for democracy. Any society must allow not only in theory, but also in practice, the possibility for fundamental changes in the social structure to take place. Taken as a principle in its concrete rather than its abstract form, the doctrine of minority rights will play an important part in any democratic theory of the future, as a protection to revolutionary forces.

Party

One of the most striking changes in the vocabulary of the new democrats is that they speak of a "movement" rather than of a "party." A movement, unlike a party, is not primarily interested in political control, but strives for social change. The democratic forces are not creating a new political party which would enter into negotiation with the traditional parties, but are building a new kind of organization which, at least until now, carries the name of "the movement." In both the East and the West, political parties are considered to be proper avenues through which political and social changes are brought about. The refusal to look upon parties or the party as instruments through which change can be brought about is part of the rejection of the liberal democratic and dialectical materialistic theories.

Many of the new democrats are members of parties and will remain, at least nominally, party members if they are permitted to do so. Many of the changes which the movement is seeking will come through party organizations, and eventually a party might be taken over by the new democrats. Indeed, the Czechoslovakian experience suggests that it is possible for a movement which has its own identity to take over a party, even though this particular attempt was crushed by foreign military intervention. In France, during the events of May 1968, it also became clear that the movement forced the Communist Party to act, even though the Party acted ineffectively and betrayed the revolutionary aims of the movement. A movement can either take over a party or force a party to act against its will.

Nevertheless, for most new democrats, the Party has become an outmoded and antiquated political institution, and in order to emphasize the break with the party form of organization, the new democrats speak of a "movement." By using this term, they emphasize the local character of the organization while still indicating certain common interests. The question of how a revolutionary movement or party can be organized is closely linked with what form of society is possible in a highly industrialized society. Today those in authority hold that the party is the only accepted form through which social and political change is possible.

Capitalism and Socialism

The new democratic theory is a socialist theory, but it refuses to discuss political and social questions primarily in terms of the formal ownership of property. To speak of democratic socialism

93

is to emphasize the fact that mere state ownership is not sufficient to ensure democracy. The new democrats look at the source of control of the means of production rather than formal ownership. In the West nationalization of the means of production, which has been the traditional demand of the socialists, has hardly been mentioned by the new democrats, even though most of them would say that they are some kind of socialist. The new democrats recognize that in a certain sense the problems faced in a socialist country and those faced in a capitalist country are similar. There is a lack of democratic control in both systems.

The terms "socialism" and "capitalism" have become increasingly unreliable in political discussion because it is not clear what the demarcation line is between a capitalist country, in which private property has long since given way to corporate capitalism, and a socialist country, in which state-owned property is operated by a bureaucratic structure. The problem of ownership is not nearly as important as the problem of control. In the nineteenth century ownership and control were generally in the same hands, and nationalization of the means of production by a democratic state was a logical and necessary demand of all socialist parties. While it is still true that the ownership and control of the means of production must pass into public hands and come under the control of the community as the first condition for a democratic political and social order, the question of formal ownership of property is not the primary issue for the new democrats. Instead, the new democrats point out the common loss of control and increasing alienation of the workers from their work in both the so-called capitalist and the so-called socialist countries. The description of individual states as either capitalist or socialist was adequate as long as there were fairly clear lines drawn between the two different kinds of political and economic systems, but the distinction between these kinds of nations is already beginning to break down, and the ways of producing are becoming more and more similar in the East and the West. Instead of speaking of socialism or capitalism, the new democrats describe nations, organizations, and communities as more or less democratic, depending upon the amount of self-control present.

Other examples of a new language which is developing to articulate the new democratic theory could be given. In addition to the specifically political language, for example, a whole new vocabulary has arisen to describe the everyday experience of young people today. When the old political language is used in new ways and when a new vocabulary arises to describe everyday experience, we have one of the clearest indications that a new theory is actually coming into being. Of course, the introduction of a new language runs the risk of breaking off communication with a significant portion of the population which speaks the old language. But the advantage is that it is possibly better to describe the kind of world in which we actually live and the alternative to the current social order. Thus, when the new democrats demand self-government in the university, in the working situation, and in the community, they do not mean that they be given representatives in the government or that they be integrated into the existing society. Instead, the new democrats mean that the institutions in which people live and work must be controlled by those who live and work in them and that the special requirements of situations must be considered in order for democracy to be meaningful.

The new democratic theory is revolutionary and goes against the whole tradition of political organization which has developed around the party structures in the East and the West.

The greatest danger of the theory is that it runs the risk of being utopian. Particularly in the United States, the new democrats sometimes fail to perceive their practice as contributing to the development of a theory and fail to see their theory to be an important part of their practice. Only if there can be a genuine unification of practice with theory, so that the theory can develop through a radical critique of existing institutions, will it be possible to construct a theory which is not utopian.

If there is to be a nonutopian democratic theory, then this theory must be Marxist, not in the sense that the theory is subservient to the party organization currently in power in communist countries, but in the sense that it understands that theory is meaningful only in relationship to practice and that practice is understandable only if it is theoretically conceived. Marx is the one political thinker and philosopher who has broken with the language and system of the past, and he is, for that reason, the most useful philosopher and political thinker for the development of a genuinely democratic theory. But the study of Marx cannot be undertaken in isolation, either from political practice or from other philosophical positions. It is crucial that we understand that almost all philosophical positions in the last few decades have attacked many of the misconceptions which Marx also rejected. Only a Marx who is interpreted radically in light of the significant philosophical and political developments since his death can be meaningful.

The greatest value of Marx's philosophy lies in his understanding that the study of politics must focus on an analysis of the concrete way in which man actually lives and that any meaningful democratic theory rejects the abstractions which have grown to dominate our lives. Indeed, as he pointed out in several places, the political institutions have turned into instruments of oppression precisely because they have become alienated and abstracted from the concrete way of life.

The new language of the new democrats is a language of praxis. It is a language of a movement searching for a fundamental social (and not merely a political) change. To speak of cooperation, of specialness, of movement, of control, and of community is to speak of situations in which man works and lives. The use of concrete language, rather than the abstractions of the past, is a practical advance which enables new problems to be discussed seriously. It is not an accident that the most pressing problem has become that of bureaucracy, for it is the bureaucracy in modern society which rules and dominates the situation in which man lives. The first and immediate attack by the new democrats has been against the bureaucratic structure. The immediate problem for the new democratic theory is to show that bureaucracy can really be brought under democratic control.

References

BRAYBROOKE, DAVID, *Three Tests for Democracy: Personal Rights, Human Welfare, Collective Preference*, Random House, New York, 1968.

> A solid attempt by a professional philosopher to make sense out of the liberal language of rights, welfare, and voting. By the tests formulated, the United States and Canada apparently fail to be democratic societies. This analysis is an example of what happens when language is discussed without reference to the material conditions or to existing social movements.

CLEAVER, ELDRIGE, *Soul on Ice*, Dell Publishing Co., New York, 1968.

> More than any other book, this best seller convinced whites that there is something special in being black and that integration would fail to solve the problems of the blacks.

The New Political Language

FANON, FRANTZ, *Black Skins; White Masks. The Experiences of a Black Man in a White World*, Grove Press, New York, 1967.

> A discussion of how the blacks are special by a native of Martinique who was educated in France and who devoted much of his short life to the revolutionary struggle for Algerian independence.

FANON, FRANTZ, *The Wretched of the Earth*, Grove Press, New York, 1966.

> An influential analysis of colonial people and of the necessity for a thorough revolution which frees the people from indirect, as well as direct, oppression by the colonizers. Fanon's arguments have been important in providing a way of understanding the special place of the blacks as a colonized people in the United States.

LIPSET, SEYMOUR, TROW, MARTIN, and COLMAN, JAMES, *Union Democracy*, Anchor Books, New York, 1962.

> This study of the internal politics of the International Typographical Union shows that the primary condition for democracy is the existence of a community. Although the assumptions of what constitutes democracy are all taken from the liberal tradition, the results of the study indicate that, in the end, a group of people must be united in a common situation in order for them to exercise real control over their lives.

THORSON, THOMAS LANDON, *The Logic of Democracy*, Holt, New York, 1962.

> An assertion of the poverty of contemporary political theory and an attempt to argue in favor of democracy. By using some of the tools of Wittgenstein, Thorson is able to show that some of the theoretical problems of the liberal democratic theory arise through faulty use of language and faulty understanding of the role and function of theory.

WHITEHEAD, ALFRED NORTH, *Science and the Modern World*, Macmillan, New York, 1925.

> In Chapter III Whitehead discusses the fallacy involved in using abstractions to describe concrete events.

7

What is to Be Done with Bureaucrats?

> *When* all *have learned to administer and actually do independently administer social production, independently keep accounts and exercise control over the parasites, the sons of the wealthy, the swindlers and other "guardians of the capitalist tradition," the escape from this popular accounting will become . . . incredibly difficult. . . .*
> LENIN

In the East and in the West there is one common practical problem which prevents the creation of a democratic society: A bureaucratic, authoritarian organizational system stands in the way of development towards the control of institutions by those who live and work in them.

An antiauthoritarian attitude is widespread among the radicals throughout the world. Much of the political work of the radicals has consisted of delegitimizing the authoritarian structure and in demonstrating that a bureaucrat can exercise his authority only so long as those under him are subservient.

What is to Be Done with Bureaucrats?

The policy of confrontation with the authoritarian system which has been pursued by the radicals, particularly in the West, has demonstrated that the survival of an authoritarian system ultimately rests on the ability of those in authority to use the police to preserve the existing power relations.

A bureaucratic system is hierarchical in nature. Although the specific form of bureaucracy depends upon the particular institution and economic system, in all bureaucratic organizations authority rests on the ability to apply coercion. The authority to apply coercion is delegated to subordinates by those at the top. In a bureaucratic system it is assumed that there must be one person or group of persons who can finally be held responsible for the system's operation. The bureaucratic system fits exactly the description which Lukacs gave of the Stalinist system: It consists of a Stalin at the top and little Stalins all the way down the line.

Ideally in a bureaucratic system decisions which explicitly limit and restrict are seldom made by those at the top. A modern authoritarian system requires the subordinates to enslave themselves. Even in a bureaucratic system people are told that they are free, but the freedom is explicitly limited by the authority which is granted to them from above. As productive agencies have become larger and larger and have taken on the form of large corporations or state-owned institutions, all pretense of a meaningful democracy in the working situation has been abandoned.

In this chapter we shall examine the failure of the traditional democratic theories to solve the problem of bureaucracy. It will be argued that the problem is not to abolish all bureaucracy but to bring bureaucratic decisions under the control of those who live and work in communities. The expansion of the working class to include many who have thought of themselves as professionals and the increasing education essential for workers in modern industrialized societies make it possible to speak of a system which is both efficient and humane. Throughout our discussion we shall assume that in order to have a democratic society in which people have real control over their lives, the authoritarian and bureaucratic organizational form must be replaced by a system based on the principle that institutions ought to be controlled by those who live and work in them. The extent to which the worker is in control of his working situation is the most essential criterion for determining whether or not a society is democratic. The new democratic theory, by focusing on the working situation rather than on the formal governmental structure, has correctly identified where the problem of establishing democracy lies. Democracy means that the worker has the power to control the decisions which affect him.

Since the implementation of a democratic and free society requires that a way to control bureaucracy be found, what to do with bureaucrats is a problem not only of political organization, but also of the nature of the social system itself. The initial reaction of many radicals was that bureaucracy must simply be destroyed and be replaced by immediate democracy. Since it was the first serious attempt to destroy the bureaucratic system, the Yugoslavian workers' council has been the model for many radicals in both the East and the West. The Yugoslavian experiment with workers' councils tried to show that an industrialized country could be created in which the workers directly made the major decisions involved in the productive process. In the past few years, however, a new form of bureaucracy has arisen in Yugoslavia and has assumed control of the institutions. Those workers with the advantage of greater experience or greater technical knowledge have been able to assume effective control of the working situation and the workers' councils have exercised little real power. The Yugoslavian experience demonstrates that bureaucracy cannot be abolished simply by declaring bureaucrats unnecessary, since experts and those who have experience are needed to make long-range plans. At least in a highly industrialized society it appears that it is not possible simply to abolish bureaucracy. The problem, rather, is to bring the decisions which are made under the effective control of the workers.

In *The New Industrial State* Galbraith describes the similarity of decision-making procedures in all industrialized societies. He shows that the way in which decisions are *actually* made is fundamentally different from the way described by the political theories held in the country. In the United States, for example, a high degree of centralization and planning are necessary and actually take place. Galbraith convincingly destroys many polular myths about the United States having a so-called free-enterprise system. The kind of planning required in the United States is not, however, the centralized planning which developed under Stalin and has since required modification. In the socialist countries it has become technically necessary for the rigid, centrally controlled state planning system to give way to a system in which managers are made responsible for decision making. It appears that some kind of decentralized planning is necessary for an efficient advanced industrial society, whether it is in the East or West.

All democratic theories, including the liberal democratic and dialectical materialistic hold that it is important for bureaucracy to be responsible to the people. However, neither in the East nor in the West has it been recognized that both planning and decentralization are necessary for an efficient social system. Instead, bureaucracy is looked upon as a necessary evil which must somehow be subordinated to the policy makers. Democratization can be brought about, it is thought, by requiring the bureaucrats to submit to the control of policy makers who are responsible to the people or to the Party.

The new democrats begin their argument against bureaucracy by noting that the liberal theory and dialectical materialism are bankrupt as descriptions of what *actually* happens and of what *ought* to happen in society. In both theories, bureaucrats or authorities have been considered to be tools which are used by those who set policies. The assumption in both positions is that knowing and doing can be sharply distinguished; some people know what ought to be done and others put into effect the decisions which are made by the superiors. Even in a bureaucracy, it is acknowledged that work is a social process, but cooperation between the superior and the subordinate is not required. In a bureaucratic system the alienation is heightened by a further sharp separation between policy makers and those who administer decisions in accordance with directives from above.

In a liberal democracy the determination of policy is placed in the hands of a congress or a president (on the government level), in the hands of a board of regents (on the university level), or in the hands of a board of directors (on the corporation level). These controlling bodies safeguard, so it is thought, the democratic nature of the institution. In a similar way, in the communist system it is argued that the Party will determine the policy at all levels. The protectors of democracy are to direct the productive process and ensure that those under them work for the benefit of society. The validity of the current democratic theories depends upon the possibility of maintaining the distinction between policy *making* and policy *implementation*. Democracy, in both the East and West, is not understood as a system in which the worker has control over the institutions in which he lives and works. It is said, however, that he can participate in the selection of representatives who supervise the control of institutions in which he works. In the liberal democracies it was thought that political regulation of economic institutions by state agencies could prevent the worst abuses of capitalism and provide democratic control of institutions. It is true that regulative agencies have had some effect; for example, they have established minimum wages and minimum health standards in factories and have provided some protection for labor unions, so that they could organize to put pressure on management for higher wages. The establishment of governmental agencies to protect the workers has, however, removed all control of the working process from the worker, since the only guarantee for the worker that minimum standards will be maintained is a new level of regulators over whom the worker exercises no control. Originally, the Communist Party was to have a similar control function in the productive process and was to ensure the maintenance of democracy. In both the liberal democracy and the communist system, however, control over the working process has been taken even further away from the worker and placed in the hands of the political bureaucracy. In both systems so-called democratization can be accomplished only by granting more power to the policy makers, who in turn can impose more control on the policy implementers.

The fallacy of the liberal democratic and dialectical materialistic positions lies in the fact that the policy maker must depend upon an administrator in order to have his policies carried out. At first glance it often looks as if the policy maker can tell the bureaucrat what to do; as a matter of fact, however, the bureaucrat determines, in the process of working, the character which the organization assumes. The bureaucratic system functions well only so long as it is not necessary for those in a subordinate position to understand the productive process. Representative bodies can control bureaucracy by determining policies for others to carry out only if it is possible to sharply separate policy making and policy implementation.

The difficulty in distinguishing between policy making and policy implementation was put by one political scientist in the following way:

Most students of public administration have discarded the old notion that administration in a government setting is distinct from policy making. Description of the policy-making cycle supports this conclusion. Policy making and administration are not only inseparable, they are indistinguishable in modern public administration. Indeed, a government agency has been defined as an organization that makes policy. A modern conception of public administration, therefore, must not merely recognize the importance of agency policy making. We have reached a point in the evolution of bureaucracy when administration must be defined explicitly in terms of the importance of policy making.[19]

But if this is true, then the argument for representative government does not hold. As is typical for most empirical studies by political scientists and sociologists on the problem of bureaucracy, their analysis destroys the presuppositions of the liberal democratic order. Bureaucracy cannot, so it seems, be controlled by granting the power of policy making to a group which is not involved in the working process. Instead of protecting the public, these policy makers themselves become a part of the bureaucracy and resist fundamental change in the decision-making procedures.

As in other cases, Marxism made a considerable theoretical advance beyond liberal democracy. The Marxists have consistently pointed out that policy making and policy implementation cannot be separated. Even when the Party was conceived of as a control institution, it was held that it could not simply lay out a position to be implemented by a group of neutral bureaucrats. Instead, the Marxists have traditionally argued that bureaucrats should simply be abolished and replaced by direct rule of the workers. As we have seen, however, the abolition of bureaucracy hardly seems any more adequate for a modern democratic society than the liberal democratic position. The abolition of bureaucracy would, indeed, solve the problem, but it does not appear to be possible to operate a productive system when everyone is allowed to make all of the decisions all of the time.

Lenin, in *State and Revolution*, has given what is perhaps the clearest exposition of the attitude which was later adopted in theory:

For when *all* have learned to administer and actually do independently administer social production, independently keep accounts and exercise control over the parasites, the sons of the wealthy, the swindlers and other "guardians of the capitalist traditions," the escape from this popular accounting and control will inevitably become so incredibly difficult, such a rare exception, and will probably be accompanied by such swift and severe punishment (for the armed workers are practical men and not sentimental intellectuals, and they will scarcely allow anyone to trifle with them) that the *necessity* of observing the simple, fundamental rules of the community will very soon become a *habit*.[20]

Lenin held that the bureaucratic functions could be reduced to merely mechanical ones, which could be performed by anyone. Control of bureaucracy would be direct, and the popular accounting of officials would be severe. The workers, once they were in control of the political system would have no need for a bureaucratic system. A system of direct democracy could be applied at all levels, which would enable those involved in the productive process to make decisions themselves. Lenin explicitly recognized that even in such a system there would be a need for technicians and engineers, and he argued that their integrity could be better maintained in enterprises controlled by the workers.

Lenin's position was accepted in theory by the dialectical materialists, although as a matter of fact a new kind of bureaucracy by the Party was created. The Party claimed to represent the true interests of the workers, and explicit orders were issued by the Party bureaucracy, which governed all aspects of life, as well as all economic matters. Every Party secretary claimed to be an expert in both theory and all practical matters. In practice, under Stalin, a bureaucracy of politically reliable directors developed who directed the affairs of the unreliable, even though in theory the Marxists have always insisted that the workers who are involved in the production know best what ought to be done.

Even though the workers have little control over their working process, the Marxist-Leninist theory, as it has been developed, insists that because the Communist Party represents the real interest of the workers, the state is still a workers' democracy. Since the Party claiming to represent the workers also controls the economic system, it automatically follows that the country is democratic. The placement of control within the Party bureaucracy precludes any effective control by the workers. In the socialist countries the situation was further complicated by the fact that the Party officials who supposedly represented the workers also often managed the productive process. The overlapping of personnel in the managers of state institutions and Party officials made a delusion of any claim for a genuine workers' democracy.

Both the liberal democratic and the dialectical materialistic positions have failed, both theoretically and practically, to solve the problem of how to control bureaucracy. Neither representative institutions nor a political party provide ways for the worker to control his working situation. The new democrats must provide a way of understanding the possibility for controlling the bureaucratic structure in an advanced industrial society. Not destruction of bureaucracy, but its control, is the crucial problem. It is both undesirable and impossible to have all decisions made by all concerned. It is desirable and possible to bring the decisions which are made under the control of those who are affected.

At this point we can assert two principles on which the control of bureaucracy rests:

1. The institution of direct democracy whenever possible;
2. Control by those affected over decisions which are made.

The first principle refers to decentralization and the practice of decision making at the lowest possible level. The second principle means that control over decisions is possible for those who are affected. Both principles are directly contrary to the bureaucratic principle, which conceives of a hierarchical structure in which authority is delegated from the top to subordinate levels within the system. In order to have a system in which bureaucracy is controlled, it is essential that authority rest in those who actually live and work in the situation concerned. Control is not merely a matter of allowing dissent to be expressed when decisions are made. Neither is it a matter of being able to elect representatives. In order to bring about real control of the decisions made, new kinds of institutions have to be created.

In some situations, particularly where work is self-directed, either individually or collectively, there is a possibility for direct democracy similar to that proposed by Lenin. In such a situation the workers are aware of the factors involved and are able to make decisions themselves. Such working situations are found in a modern society more frequently than is often realized. One of the most effective ways to bring bureaucracy under control is to increase the amount of work which can be self-directed and to abolish the bureaucracy in such situations. For example, in universities it may be possible to bring about a maximum amount of self-direction by the workers because of a greater awareness of factors involved in the working process. In other institutions and in factories it will be necessary to enlarge the scope of work done by the worker so that bureaucracy may be brought under control. Job enlargement which will enable the worker to have greater understanding of his place in the productive process is one of the most important prerequisites for decentralization and for the institution of direct democracy.

In many working situations the tasks which are given to the workers come from outside, but the working process itself can be determined by those directly involved. Even in factories where a considerable amount of detail work is necessary, it is possible for units within the productive process to have some kind of autonomy with regard to the decisions on how the work will be done. The efficiency of the working process increases as the workers assume more control over the working situation. Originally centralization was a necessity for efficient operation of an economic system, but it has begun to be a hindrance. In an advanced industrial society in which we find increasing automation and constant technical improvement, it is necessary for creativity to be encouraged on the part of an increasing number of workers. No longer is a good worker one who always does what he is told. He is expected to understand and know the working process in which he participates. This is possible, however, only if he is freed from oppressive direction from above. The hierarchical structure proves to be inefficient in a productive process which requires creativity on the part of the workers.

Management theory has begun to reflect this decisive change in the productive process; it is now argued that a certain amount of decentralization is essential if efficiency is to be maintained. In the socialist countries, the realization that decentralization is a technical necessity once the economic system has begun to function well has provided the most powerful impetus for recent economic reforms. However, as long as the decentralization process merely means the decision making will be shifted from higher management to lower management, there will be no significant democratization. The full benefits of decentralization will come when it is consequently carried out, and the worker assumes significant control over management decisions. To decentralize does not mean that management will become obsolete, but rather that management will give up its oppressive role and take over the function of representing the worker in his relationship to the world outside the productive process. Management will be under the control of those in the productive process.

Although it is already generally recognized that a certain amount of decentralization is necessary for efficient operation, the reasons for this decisive change in the organization of the work process have hardly been noticed. When the valuable worker participates creatively in the social process of work, bureaucracy hinders, rather than helps. In a highly industrialized system the worker is required to be increasingly better trained and educated. Productivity is advanced by improving the ability of the workers to create and manipulate the means of production. A new kind of worker, who is well educated and creative in his working process, is in increasing demand as industrialization proceeds.

The demand for well-educated and trained workers has stimulated increasing bureaucratization in the university. The bureaucratic structure has been transferred to the university. Administrators treat the teachers and researchers as hired hands, while the students are looked upon as products which must be turned out and marketed. As has already been stated in Chapter 5, recent events in universities clearly indicate that the educated researchers and teachers are becoming part of the working class, which has interests fundamentally different from those of the administrators. At the same time it has been recognized that universities, if they are to be good, must allow a considerable degree of self-government. Furthermore, if the faculty members and researchers are to do their jobs well, the university must assure them freedom for personal development. Actually the conditions necessary for research have become freer in many private and governmental research institutes than in the university. This process is particularly so in Central Europe, where the members of the academies of science (the research institutions in most communist countries) enjoy a relatively high degree of freedom while the university personnel are held to a much stricter test of political reliability.

The revolt of many intellectuals is an assertion of the necessity for them to control their working situation. They are not special people who consider themselves entitled to more freedom on the basis of their specialness, but they are workers who need more freedom in order to produce well. In the long run, however, their struggle for democracy will not be successful unless there is a fundamental change in the nature of the economic and political order, which will enable all workers to control their working situations. If democracy is to be advanced, and if a truly efficient society is to be created, the encouragement of decentralization and individuality must be accelerated in every working situation.

The term *worker* still means a creative individual who takes part in the productive process, whose only property is his labor time. But the new members of the working class are people who are not considered workers in this traditional sense, i.e., the unskilled persons who have nothing to sell but their labor time and who generally perform menial functions. The working class includes an increasingly large number of people who once thought of themselves as independent professionals with control over their lives but who have recently been treated more and more as workers in the traditional sense. As already mentioned, this changing relationship of the professionals to those in power is most strikingly evident at the universities, in both the East and the West. But the bureaucratic pattern of organization is prevalent in other institutions also, so that changes are occurring in the working situations of other professionals as well (for example, among elementary and secondary school teachers, nurses, doctors, engineers, and so on). It is symptomatic that some of these groups of workers are beginning to turn to the organizational form traditionally used by the working class: the union. This movement, however, will have to become a part of a much larger movement which unites all of those who are treated as wage laborers in the present order, or it will be impotent. The rule of the working classes, which is a part of any democratic program, requires not only decentralization, but also control over the bureaucracy.

In order for a system to be democratic, it is not sufficient for the workers to determine how their work will be accomplished within a framework which is imposed upon them. The workers must have control over the important production decisions, and their production must meet genuine human needs. In the contemporary industrial society, productive decisions are determined in accordance with the interests of those in power. In a capitalist society, for example, where the market has influence on the productive process, what will be produced is determined by those who control the advertising and distribution systems. In the centrally planned, socialist state, what will be produced is determined by the political interests of those in power.

Control of bureaucracy is not only a problem within productive units, but also a question of the general organization of society and how priorities are established by society. Bureaucracy will not be brought under control and democracy will not be present until the workers can participate in organizing their working situation and can determine the kind of production which will take place.

Since the political structure and the economic structure are intertwined, any new democratic theory must emphasize that the economic system—the conditions under which work is done—must be democratized. The new democratic theory is a socialist theory which does not place primary emphasis on the nationalization of industries or on the creation of state-owned economic units. It is socialist, rather, in its demand that the process of work be brought under the control of the workers. The new democratic theory recognizes that the important questions lie in the decentralization of authority and the creation of institutions which are controlled by those engaged in the productive process. It is clear that this theory must also advocate the abolition of private property, if "property" is understood as being that which stands under the control of nonpublic forces. The new democratic theory is socialist in the truest and most fundamental sense.

What is to Be Done with Bureaucrats?

The new industrial system requires workers who can work cooperatively. Individual responsibility, which characterizes the hierarchically organized system, is increasingly being replaced by group responsibility. The socialization of the working process is furthered by the increasingly complicated nature of work, which requires an educated and creative worker who realizes his special capabilities within a social situation. The socialized individual is necessary for the development of an efficient industrial system. If efficiency is understood not only in terms of the number of units produced, but also in terms of the quality of production, understanding on the part of the worker is even more important. Humanization of the working process is becoming essential for a productive economic system. The new democratic theory, with its emphasis on control of the working situation by those involved, is therefore a theory for an advanced industrial society.

The Hungarian sociologist Andras Hegedus has argued that it is necessary for optimalization and humanization to proceed together. In the long run the most efficient society will be a humanized one. Narrowness of education, control of the press, and specialization of the working process to inhibit worker control can, in the short run, enable the production of large numbers of goods. Such a system, however, dehumanizes the workers and prevents them from participating in the working process in the manner which is necessary for them to be truly efficient workers. The control of bureaucracy, through decentralization and through the establishment of control institutions, is necessary for both an efficient and humane economic system. It is obvious that a nonbureaucratic system is more humane; it appears that it is becoming more efficient. The dual demands of optimal efficiency and maximum humanization are complementary, rather than contradictory.

114

What is to Be Done with Bureaucrats?

A fundamental tension arises in situations where the worker must be creative to work well but where he still must work within an authoritarian system. Those workers who must be creative to work well are the source of much of the opposition to the authoritarian system today. The teachers, nurses, and other professionals who are forming unions are seeking not only increased wages, but also asking for control over their working situations. The revolt within the university is perhaps best understood as a reaction to the changing character of the working population. The university student today, particularly in a large university, has two contradictory demands placed upon him: He is required to be creative, and this creativity is a necessary prerequisite for success in the university and later as a worker. And in addition to being creative, it is demanded that he be docile, that he look upon his education as a training to assume his place in the existing social order, and that he, both as a potential worker and as a human being, submit himself to the discipline of an authoritarian structure. A democratic education would not be only a highly specialized training for one position, but would also include knowledge which would allow the worker to understand and critically evaluate the nature of the system in which he works. Much of the student revolt at the universities has been against the narrow conception of education as a process of acquiring technical skills which enable one to be useful to the existing order. The state universities in the United States, in particular, are primarily large training centers for the capitalist system, but these same universities are also proving to be the training ground for the new democrats, who insist on a radical revision of the university and of society. Precisely because creativity and docility are incompatible, the university has become the center of the revolt against the bureaucratic structure and one of the

centers of the developing new democratic theory. But the
tensions within the university are only a taste of the tensions
present within the skilled professions in an advanced industrial
society. The authoritarian system, when it is continued in an
advanced industrial society, creates its own contradictions.
The movement recognizes this phenomenon in the phrase, "the
system creates its own radicals."

Traditional liberal democrats have argued that bureaucracy
can be controlled through representative institutions; the
traditional Leninists have argued that bureaucracy can be
abolished and that bureaucrats can be replaced by unskilled
workers. Representation has been shown to be merely an
illusion, since the problem is not to participate in all decisions,
but to exercise effective control over those who make decisions.
Nor has a disciplined party membership proved to be an
effective means of controlling the productive institutions.
In practice, neither of the methods which have been tried by
those arguing for liberal democracy or dialectical materialism
have led to effective and humane control of bureaucracy. By
rejecting the distinction between policy maker and policy
implementer, the new democrats have opened up the possibility
for the development of control institutions in an advanced
industrial society.

In order to achieve democratic control over the means of
production, it is necessary for communities to be created which
have real power. In the following chapters we shall discuss the
nature of the alienation which exists and how this alienation
can be overcome, and then we shall turn to the problem of the
creation of communities in which the workers can exercise
effective control over the means of production.

References

ARGYRIS, CHRIS, *Personality and Organization. The Conflict Between System and the Individual,* Harper, New York, 1957.
> A discussion of the informal organizational structures which frustrate the bureaucratic system. Although the book is written to encourage a "human relations" approach, which in the end is merely another way to manipulate individuals, it does show that a bureaucratic system is not efficient and that the most efficient system is one in which individuals develop what Argyris calls "healthy" personalities.

BERGER PETER (ed), *Marxism and Sociology: Views from Eastern Europe,* Appleton-Century-Crofts, New York, 1969.
> A collection of articles by Central European Marxist sociologists. Of particular interest to this discussion is an article by Hegedus, "The Division of Labor and the Social Structure of Socialism."

BOYER, WILLIAM W., *Bureaucracy on Trial. Policy Making by Government Agencies,* Bobbs-Merrill, Indianapolis, 1964.
> Boyer gives a good analysis of problems of bureaucracy in government agencies. He concludes that the only way to overcome bureaucracy is to increase the power of those at the top.

CROZIER, MICHEL, *The Bureaucratic Phenomenon,* University of Chicago Press, 1964.
> An excellent discussion, by a Frenchman, of the bureaucratic phenomenon. Particularly relevant to our discussion is the description of the changes, over time, which have taken place in the nature of bureaucracy and the way in which a bureaucratic system impedes the efficient operation of an industrialized system (see pp. 178–208).

GERTH, H. H., and MILLS, C. WRIGHT, *From Max Weber: Essays in Sociology,* Oxford University Press, New York, 1946.
> Weber was the first to describe the phenomenon of bureaucracy, and his influence has been decisive in most empirical studies of the bureaucratic phenomenon. Weber sought to improve on Marx, but his analysis is weakest when it comes to the problem of how bureaucracy can be combatted.

GOULDNER, ALVIN W., *Patterns of Industrial Bureaucracy,* The Free Press, Glencoe, Ill., 1954.
> A classic study of bureaucracy and the way in which lower levels avoid and modify attempts at regulation by the "policy makers."

What is to Be Done with Bureaucrats?

This book is a good description of how bureaucratic machinery functions.

KOLAJA, JIRI, *Workers' Councils. The Yugoslav Experience*, Praeger, New York, 1966.

A short book describing the workers' councils in Yugoslavia. The study is based on a very limited visit to Yugoslavia in 1959 and does not take into account the experience of the workers' councils over an extended period, but it is still a valuable introduction for the American reader.

WARD, BENJAMIN N., *The Socialist Economy. A Study of Organizational Alternatives*, Random House, New York, 1967.

Although the book is often technical in nature and treats economic systems in their pure forms, it is still possible for the untrained reader to see various alternatives for a socialist society. Of particular relevance to this chapter are the discussions of the Soviet and Yugoslav economic systems.

8
Overcoming Alienation

> *The community from which the worker is isolated is a
> community which belongs to an entirely different reality and
> is of an entirely different scope than the political community.
> This community, from which his own work separates him,
> is life itself—physical and intellectual life, human morality,
> human activity, human enjoyment, human nature.*
> MARX

The primary practical aim of the new democrats has been to
work for new ways of achieving democracy by decentralization
and control of bureaucracy. The primary theoretical problem
is the nature of alienation and how it can be overcome.

Theoretically and practically, the concept of alienation has
played an important role in the development of the radical
position. A sense of alienation from the existing order is important for any movement which is working for fundamental
change in society. One of the most important tasks of the new
democrats is to point out and attack alienation in all of its
appearances in contemporary society. A political movement
which aims at fundamental social change is possible today
because a large number of people experience a deep and pro-

found sense of alienation from the political and social order. The appearance of alienation is one of the best indications that man has lost control of the situations in which he lives and works. The success of the movement will depend upon how effectively it can mobilize the widespread, but often poorly organized, sections of the population which find the life they lead to be unsatisfactory. It must be shown that alienation is a social, not a personal, problem which exists among those who do not control their working situation.

The concept of alienation was first used in its contemporary sense by Marx, in what has come to be known as the "Economic and Philosophic Manuscripts."[21] These manuscripts, which Marx wrote at the age of twenty-six, were not published until 1932. In them he used alienation in the tradition of the important English political economists of his time, particularly Smith and Ricardo. For them, alienation was the act of transferring the products of one's labor to another person, and it was a necessity in an industrialized society. Man must alienate his products and turn them into commodities. For the English political economists, economics is the study of the production and exchange of commodities. Alienation of human labor, that is the creation of a system of wage labor, is a necessary part of the capitalist system.

Marx broadened the discussion of alienation to include a description of the social life which develops in a society based upon the sale (alienation) of human labor. He perceived work as the fundamental activity of man and the expression of man's creativity as a social human being. Alienated labor arises when man's labor time is objectified as a commodity which can be traded and sold. The proletariat, according to Marx, is the class of wage earners who have no property but their labor, which they must alienate from themselves in order to be

120

productive. Work, for Marx, is not merely an unwelcome necessity; it is a human activity important for its own sake. Labor time cannot be exchanged for material goods without dehumanizing the worker. An economic system, such as capitalism, which is based on the transfer of the control of human labor time is, in its very essence, dehumanizing.

What has come to be called Marx's "humanism" is derived from the recognition that the concept of alienation is useful to describe not only the basic transaction of an economic system based on private property, but also the dehumanization of man when he lacks control over his working situation. Much of Marx's analysis of alienation was influenced by Hegel and Feuerbach, two philosophers who described it (*Entfremdung*) as a process in which man loses his basic humaneness. For Hegel and Feuerbach alienation was not conceived of as an economic category, but as a description of the lostness and estrangement which man experiences in the world where true humaneness is lacking.

Marx understood that alienation as described by the English political economists and by Feuerbach refers to essentially the same phenomenon. The economic process of selling one's labor time requires the seller to treat his own creativity as a foreign object. The act of production, which is the most fundamental human activity, is removed from the control of man when labor time becomes a commodity.

Alienation, then, as it was analyzed by Marx, is the state in which man is separated from his activity as a creative human being. This separation, in the capitalist system, took place when large numbers of people who had only their labor time to sell were mobilized to work in factories. Alienated labor has been extended as the factory form of organization has been transferred to other institutions.

Overcoming Alienation

In the *Theorien über den Mehrwert* (*Theories of Surplus Value*), in a passage written when he was more mature, Marx distinguished himself sharply from those whom he called the "sentimental opponents" of capitalism. Marx, like other communists of his day, argued that alienated labor could be abolished only by abolishing private property. Marx worked out his own position, in contrast to that of the utopian communists, by developing his relationship to the work of Ricardo, one of the chief theoreticians of capitalism:

Ricardo correctly (for his time) considered the capitalist form of production to be the most advantageous and the most suitable for producing wealth. Ricardo wants *production for the sake of production*, and he is correct in wanting this. If one wants to claim as the sentimental opponents of Ricardo have done, that production is not in itself the goal, then one forgets that production for the sake of production means nothing else than the development of human powers of production. . . . That is to say, it means nothing else than the *development of the richness of human nature for its own sake*. . . . It is not understood that this development of the capacities of the species *Man*, although it is at first brought about at the cost of the majority of human individuals and certain classes, finally breaks through this antagonism and the social development coincides with the development of the single individual, and that therefore the higher development of individuality can be bought only by an historical process in which individuals are sacrificed.[22]

In this complicated and sometimes awkward passage Marx argued that it is wrong to oppose capitalism in a sentimental way, since capitalism tremendously increased the productive capabilities of society. This increase of social productivity came about by creating an economic system in which production is done for its own sake and not for immediate use, but this progress was possible only through the suffering of the working class. Marx argued, and it is being shown today, that the process of production for production's sake will require that man, as an individual, develop his powers, just as society has tremendously increased its productivity.

Objectification, that is the process of producing for its own sake, must be distinguished from alienation, when work is done for another. Both objectification of work and the alienation of work are the historic results of capitalism. It is objectification, however, and not alienation which is necessary and desirable in the modern industrial process. It is true that alienation will not be overcome by allowing each worker to "do his own thing," since the productive process has become cooperative and socialized. In a democratic society, however, where alienation is overcome, the working process comes under the collective control of the workers, and individual and social development can proceed together.

Marx analyzed four different forms of alienation of the worker which appear in a system based on private property: alienation from his product, from the working process, from his own creativity, and from his fellow man. The most obvious form of alienation is the estrangement of the worker from the product of his labor. In the act of production, the worker produces for another who has purchased his labor time. The product of his work is estranged from himself and is not considered to be his product. The worker has no stake in the product, but is interested only in receiving wages in exchange for his working time.

The estrangement from the products of one's labor also means that the working process itself becomes a foreign process over which the worker has no control. Not only is the product foreign to him, but also the way in which the product is produced is foreign to him and under the control of another. The working conditions, the speed of the work, and the particular way the work is done are not controlled by the worker, but are determined by a foreign agent. In a manufacturing system (which is an early form of industrialization) this separation of the worker from the process of working is particularly well developed. In the manufacturing system, the working process is completely beyond the control of the worker, who becomes a part of the assembly line.

The separation of the worker from his product and from the productive process means in addition that the worker is alienated from himself as a creative person. In his working process he is not a person who creates; instead he works for the time when he can be free from work. In its early stages the labor movement put great emphasis on the reduction of the working day so that the worker could be freed from forced labor. It was assumed that the worker could be a creative person in his free time. As we shall see later, the modern industrial society ceases to recognize the distinction between working time and free time and attempts to extend the power of these who control the productive process into what has traditionally been considered to be free time.

The alienation from the product of work, the process of working, and the creative activity of the worker results in an alienation of the worker from his fellow man. In the manufacturing and industrial systems the worker becomes socialized to a degree never before accomplished in the history of mankind. In the production process the individual worker is dependent on his fellow workers in order to be productive. But in the manufacturing situation, in which the worker is alienated from his product, the working process, and from himself, the worker cannot have a genuine relationship with his fellow workers, since they are forced to treat each other as objects. Cooperation of the workers as men and not merely as objects engaged in production comes about only when they stand together and organize to oppose the system which dominates their lives. In the process of organizing in opposition to the system in which they live and work, the workers begin to develop a genuine relationship with one another as creative human beings. But this relationship exists only in opposition to the system in which they find themselves.

The concept of alienation has become fashionable since the rediscovery of Marx's early writings. Today alienation has become part of the vocabulary of science and of everyday life. Often, however, alienation is understood primarily as a kind of feeling that the individual is lost and alone in the world. The discussion has focused less on the nature of the working process and more on what is called "free" time. But an increasing number of young people are coming to realize that it is nearly impossible to develop freely unless the pressures which they encounter in the consumer-oriented society can be removed. Many of these young people drop out of society. The dropout phenomenon, which is claiming so many of the most intelligent and most promising members of society, indicates how total the alienation from the existing social order has become for a substantial proportion of the young people in the capitalist world.

If alienation is conceptualized merely as a feeling of lostness, however, there is little alternative but to treat it as a kind of illness. Alienation can be overcome, if it is understood as a psychological state, by changing the state of mind. The state of mind can be changed by taking drugs, by dropping out of society, or by getting assistance from a psychiatrist. The widespread experimentation with drugs will continue as long as alienation is understood as a state of mind.

Today's alienation has manifested itself in many different forms. The power of the concept of alienation comes from the fact that it unites a description of the working process in the modern industralized nations with a description of man as a human being who has lost control over his vital activity. The tendency on the part of those who serve as apologists for the existing order is to turn alienation into a concept which describes how one feels about the world. Alienation of human labor in the working process, it is thought, is necessary for all societies. The best that can be hoped for is that the attitude which men take toward their lives can be changed. If alienation is to be a meaningful social concept, however, it must describe the actual life of man and not merely his feelings.

As long as labor is treated as a commodity which can be bought and sold, the Marxian analysis is still valid. In all countries dominated by the liberal democrats and in the socialist countries of Europe, the worker is still treated primarily as a commodity. The proletariat is the class of all those who sell their labor as a commodity; the capitalist class consists of those who purchase the labor of others in order to increase the quantity of capital. Marx's definition of the proletariat fits nearly all of the intellectuals and students today who have no other product to sell than their skill; the alienation which they have felt is merely an extension of that which has been widespread in the traditional working class. Marx correctly understood that the relationship between the capitalist and the worker dominated the social order in the nineteenth century and that this relationship produced deep-seated ambiguities which made the economic and social system of the nineteenth century intrinsically unstable and transitory.

When man's labor is alienated, he loses control over one of his most important activities: the process of working. He can no longer be in control of his creativity, but can only sell himself to be used by another. Only by socializing his work (which has already happened in the most advanced industrial societies) and by controlling his working process as a *social* process can he overcome alienation. An efficient economic system is one in which the unalienated man engages in his work for its own sake and not because he has sold himself to another. Work, as a social process, will continue to be a process of objectification, but when it comes under the control of the worker, alienation can be overcome. Alienation, for Marx, is rooted in the system of private property, for in this system, man and the products of man's labor are treated as objects. The sense of estrangement, or alienation, can be overcome only if the economic fact of human beings having to sell their labor as a commodity is eliminated. The selling of labor time can be overcome only if the system of private property and commodity exchange are abolished. Socialization of the means of production is a necessary prerequisite for overcoming alienation.

Alienation is the result of the form of societal organization in which man is treated merely as an object. In political terms, alienation can best be understood as the state in which the citizen exercises no control over his fate but is treated as a thing to be manipulated by others. The state in which alienation is present is the one in which democracy is absent.

In the previous chapter we began to see that the classical form of bureaucracy applied to the early forms of the manufacturing system. We saw also that the industrial system is beginning to require a more creative kind of worker. It is becoming increasingly clear that the best workers are those who are not alienated from their products, their process of working, themselves, and their fellow human beings. To be truly productive, once a higher level of productivity is reached, it is essential that the conditions of alienation in the working process be removed. To remove these conditions completely, however, a fundamental change in the system of property relations is necessary. Only in a democratic society in which alienation can be overcome can production increase continuously. Only there can individual and social development be brought into line.

Alienation, as it was seen by Marx, was primarily present in the immediate working situation. In an advanced industrial society it is becoming increasingly important for those in authority to control and influence man's free time, when he consumes the product of social labor, as well as his working time. Free time has come under the control of those who dominate the working situation as the consumption of products has become important for determining what will be produced. The so-called consumer-oriented society treats man in his free time as an object to be manipulated and used by those in control of the economic system. For Marx the struggle against alienation was the struggle against the long working day. He saw the shortening of the working day as the first step toward the establishment of the reign of freedom. A Marxist discussion of the problem of alienation today cannot be carried out merely by gathering quotations from Marx, since alienation is now present in all areas of man's life. Socialism (control of the working process) is a necessary, but is apparently not a sufficient, condition for overcoming alienation in a society in which nonworking time is no longer free time.

Both in the Stalinist era, in which dialectical materialism was developed, and in the advanced stages of capitalism, in which liberal democracy has developed, an increasing control of man's free time has taken place. Under Stalin the control of free time was direct and sometimes brutal. Man's whole life was a subject of manipulation to be determined by what would benefit society. What would benefit society was defined by the

Party, which was controlled by Stalin. The Stalinist system required, both theoretically and practically, that the control of man's time be extended as far as possible. Instead of abolishing alienation, the Stalinist method of turning private property into state property merely generalized and deepened alienation. No matter where or when one might be acting, one was subject to control by the authorities. Marx's description of the plight of the worker in the nineteenth century could be matched by descriptions of the everyday life of the citizen living in a Stalinist system.

In the advanced capitalist society, the encroachment upon free time has been more subtle but equally widespread. Theoretically, the change to what is called the consumer-oriented society has been heralded as an advance of democracy by the liberal democrats. This consumer-oriented, new form of society is one in which the comsumption of goods becomes an important determinant of what is to be produced. Indeed, a large proportion of the efforts of corporations is aimed at creating needs where none have been present and in manipulating the public so that the products which have been produced so efficiently can be sold. Of course, there is nothing wrong with the consumption of products if they meet real human needs and meet them well. But in the so-called consumer-oriented society goods are produced primarily to be sold, not to be used. The exchange value, rather than the use value, of the product determines what will be produced. This is true whether we are speaking of razor blades, cars, or presidential candidates.

We are robbed of our free time in at least two ways in the consumer-oriented society. First, during a substantial part of our time we are being enticed to purchase products. The mass media become little more than carriers of advertising, and the content of what is printed and broadcast is determined primarily by its acceptability to advertisers. Whether we like it or not, our time is taken away from us as we are constantly assaulted by demands for our attention and money. Second, the products which we *do* buy all too often turn out to have been produced merely to be sold. The façade quickly wears out, and we must spend our time to maintain or replace them.

In addition, control over the means of production in capitalism has become centered in a relatively small number of corporations which can successfully manipulate the consumer. These corporations are closely linked to the military, and much of their production has been geared to supplying the needs of the government. The government has become one of the largest consumers, and there is an overlapping of personnel between those who control the government and those who control the productive process.

Throughout this development of a consumer-oriented society alienation has increased. The alienation has been expressed not only in working time, but in what was thought to be free time as well. The loss of control over one's life has extended beyond the working situation, so that today both the working situation and the so-called free time have become dominated by alienation.

Working time has begun to be reduced to the point where in some instances, more time is free than is spent working. An analysis of man's life today must focus on the concrete possibilities for the development of man's creativity both during working hours and in that part of the day which is now said to be free. Control by those in authority has been extended, and alienation has grown as the working day has been shortened. In addition to forced labor, we now have forced activity during free time. Coercion is applied by those in authority to make man's activity during his free time serve the interests of those in control of the means of production.

The productive process is still primary, and the control over free time has increased because of the demands of those in control of the means of production. In order to overcome alienation, whether during working time or during free time, it is necessary to bring man's labor time under the control of the workers. By doing this, man's free time can be truly freed from the domination of those who control him. Genuine free time will exist only when the worker exercises control over his working situation.

Marx's analysis of alienation has played a particularly important role in many of the recent theoretical discussions in the Central European countries. This is partly owing to the fact that the early writings of Marx were not published until 1932, nearly a decade after Lenin's death. By that time the official dialectical materialist position had already been formulated, and no significant change in the official position was permitted. Moreover, no significant scholarship on Marx was done as long as Stalinism was the dominant force. The early manuscripts in which alienation was discussed were first ignored by Stalinists and later condemned as immature and unrepresentative works of Marx. The early writings were not included in the official editions of Marx's works, and only after they began to be discussed in the West did they become available in the communist world.

Many West European and Yugoslavian Marxists opened the discussion of the role of alienation in Marx's works. More recently in Central Europe this discussion has taken on practical importance. The official dialectical materialist position held that alienation was certainly present in the capitalist nations still based on private property, but that any discussion of the presence of alienation in the socialist countries called into question the success of the revolution. Those who recognize that alienation still exists in socialist countries were required to openly combat the claim that dialectical materialism is the only correct interpretation of Marxism.

Mihaly Vajda has summarized the Hungarian discussion of alienation in *Praxis*, 1967.[23] The position of Vajda, a member of the Lukacs group in Hungary, might be taken as representative of the position taken by many of those who have argued for increased democratization. After briefly recapitulating the basic positions held during the discussion, Vajda concludes that Marx's discussion of alienation must be taken as a significant part of his writings and that any important analysis of the socialist society to be developed in Hungary must recognize the presence of alienation. Indeed, he gives what might well be one of the best criteria for the development of a true democracy when he states that a true communist society is one in which alienation has actually been overcome. According to this interpretation, the current stage of socialism is a transition phase from an alienated to an unalienated society, and communism will be achieved only when the condition of alienation present in society has been overcome.

To develop an unalienated society in the socialist countries, where large-scale private property has long since disappeared, greater control by the workers over the productive process must be gained. The decentralization of the economic system has been supported by those in Central Europe who have argued that a socialist society must overcome alienation. These democrats, however, have insisted that the democratization must be carried further than any proposals made by the current leadership.

The concept of alienation, whether it is understood as a lack of control over the working situation or, in the extended sense, as a lack of control over free time, provides a way of conceptualizing the basic fault of the life created in the advanced industrialized societies. Control of the working situation is necessary for alienation to be overcome, and control of the working situation by those involved in the productive process will enable free time to be freed from an oppressive system. The sense of dissatisfaction which is felt so widely in the world today is not the result of a personal failure by many people to adjust, but is an indication that the social order has produced an unsatisfactory kind of life.

Alienation is the most personal form in which the new democrats understand the world in which they live. But this personal alienation from the society can be overcome only by creating democratic institutions which are under the control of the workers. To create a democracy, for the new democrats, is to overcome alienation. To control bureaucracy is but one necessary step in this direction. The general problem raised by the new democrats is how a new world and social order can be created in which there can be a life of social praxis controlled by those engaged in production.

References

BLAUNER, ROBERT, *Alienation and Freedom. The Factory Worker and His Industry*, University of Chicago Press, 1964.

> An extremely valuable study of the main types and degrees of alienation in industry. Blauner concludes that as automation increases alienation can be (but not necessarily must be) overcome by giving more control to the worker. He also shows that efficiency increases as the worker achieves more control over his working situation.

CHINOY, ELY, *Automobile Workers and the American Dream*, Doubleday, New York, 1955.

> A study of automobile workers which shows how alienation extends over both the working and free time and how the workers attempt to

make do in a difficult situation. This book is a good antidote to those who claim that the workers in the United States live happy and fulfilling lives and have no interest in a system in which they exercise real control over their activities.

FRIEDMANN, GEORGES, *The Anatomy of Work. Labor, Leisure and the Implications of Automation*, translated by Wyatt Rawson, The Free Press, New York, 1961.

A warm and human, yet rigorous, discussion of the possibility for the humanization of labor. Of particular interest are the discussions of specialization, the possibility for job enlargement, and the relationship of free time to working time. The thesis that humanization of labor is necessary for real efficiency is developed.

KENNISTON, KENNETH, *The Uncommitted*, Harcourt, New York, 1965.

Kenniston shows the many forms which alienation takes among youth in the United States. He defines alienation as, "an explicit rejection, 'freely' chosen by the individual of what he perceives as the dominant values or norms of his society" (p. 455).

MARCUSE, HERBERT, *One-Dimensional Man. Studies in the Ideology of Advanced Industrial Society*, Beacon Press, Boston, 1964.

Marcuse's greatest contribution is his description of the oppression present in advanced capitalism. His early influence on the movement has nearly vanished because he failed to provide an adequate analysis of forces seeking genuine social change. In the end, Marcuse's argument is for dropping out of the system, and his social protest leads to what he calls a "Great Refusal," rather than to participation in the revolutionary movement.

9
A Society
Fit to Live in

"What should be" is therefore concrete, and is moreover the
only realistic and historic interpretation of reality; it is the
only active history and philosophy, the only politics.
GRAMSCI

A democratic society is one in which alienation is overcome and
bureaucracy is brought under control. The revolutionary
movement begins with a critical analysis of the existing order
and focuses on fundamental change. A democratic movement,
however, goes beyond criticism. Its purpose is to create a
society fit to live in, a social order in which individuals and
communities can develop to the fullest extent. A vision of a
world other than the one in which we live is inherent in
revolutionary theory. Such a vision is not utopian so long as it
expresses 'he real desires and demands of the people who live
and work as a part of society.

The program of the new democrats is based on their analysis
of the society in which they live. They do not long for a better
place in another part of the world, and it makes no sense to
tell them to leave if they don't like the society in which they

135

live. The new democrats look at their own society as one which has the potential of being a place where they can live as free human beings. Particularly in the earlier stages of the movement, those rebelling against the current order sometimes seemed to be motivated by a rejection of the technological society and a desire for a return to a simple life. As the theory and practice of the movement have developed, however, it has become clear that the problem is not to escape from society, but to take hold of the societies in which we live and to bring them under the control of the people. The concept of community control over the working and living situation has developed as the center of the democratic theory, and as the movement has progressed, there has been a growing realization that a democratic society can exist in an advanced industrialized world if it is based on the rule of the workers.

Dissatisfaction with the successful life and a sense of alienation are widespread in all of the advanced industrialized countries. The societies in which we now live are not fit to live in. The United States is an imperialist and racist nation. The comforts of the industrialized world are provided by the oppressed peoples of the world. The universities, which ought to serve the people, instead play an important role in sustaining the imperialist and racist social order. Professors often drop out into their own comfortable homes and exist as apologists and ideologists of the system. In Central and Eastern Europe, even though a form of socialism has been achieved, alienation and bureaucracy are still a part of man's everyday life. To speak of a society fit to live in is to speak of a society which is fundamentally different from the one which now exists.

It has become clear that revolutionary change requires a qualitative and not merely a quantitative change in society. The sons and daughters of the middle class are recognizing their

136

allies to be the poor and oppressed throughout the world, not because they feel sorry for those who are said to be less fortunate than they, but because they see their own liberation to be possible only if a democratic society can be created. They have seen that they are culturally deprived despite their material wealth. The values of hard work and integration have been challenged and are being replaced by a desire to develop the special characteristics of communities.

The development of communities is the alternative to the futile search for individual liberation in an unfree society. The problem of developing communities is to create a qualitatively new kind of life. In the advanced industrial nations of the world today communities are being systematically destroyed, and their destruction is an important part of the enslaving process.

A society fit to live in is one in which communities are developed, rather than destroyed. A true community is composed of individuals who live and work in a common situation. Community life is developed insofar as the special interests of the community and the members of the community are developed. A community is based on the everyday life of man as an active, working being, and the goal of the democratic movement is to create a society based on communities organized around the real life of man. A community cannot be aggressive and imperialistic if it is based on developing the specialness of the members of the community. A community relates to other communities, but in order to preserve its own special characteristics it does not seek to dominate and absorb the lives of others. Such a vision of the community as the basic social unit is wishful thinking unless it is bound to a movement which learns through its revolutionary praxis what the real possibilities are for the development of communities in the twentieth century. Those who ask what contemporary revolutionaries want must be satisfied with the answer that they want a life which is fit to live. This is a life in which quality is important and community life is real.

Individual liberation apart from the revolutionary movement, whether it is attempted by dropping out of the system or by dropping out through being caught up in the system, is insufficient to create a democratic society. Individual liberation from a dull and tiresome life has been the traditional hope and desire of the members of the so-called middle class who are caught in the intolerable situation of identifying with the ruling class even though they have no real common interest with it. The development of "flower children" among the families of the middle class is a testimony to the bankruptcy of the lives of their parents. As these flower children realize that their own liberation is possible only if society can be fundamentally changed, they become a part of the democratic movement. Attempted individual liberation, whether it is by hard work, by the aid of a psychiatrist, or by escaping from society will remain a luxury of those who are members of the ruling class. The hope for individual liberation has kept the members of the middle class enslaved and can keep them from recognizing that their real interests lie with the revolutionary movement.

A democratic society today requires social experimentation and praxis in a way never before attempted. Experiments in new forms of living, including new forms of family life and working situations, are an important part of the everyday life of the new democrats. But while new forms of personal relations are essential, if the arrangement of a more "meaningful" life remains the privilege of the middle class, these experiments will be futile unless a movement for a revolutionary change in society is developed. We must not only conceptualize, but we must begin to create and implement alternative systems and alternative means for organizing a productive society. If the test of efficiency is extended to include the quality, as well as the quantity of objects produced, a productive society is one which produces not only better goods, but also better men, who are able to control their own lives.

A genuine democracy aspires to the standard set in the discussion in Plato's *Republic*, where democracy is described as the most varied and rich form of life:

What, then said I, is the manner of their life and what is the quality of such a democratic constitution? For it is plain that the man of this quality will turn out to be a democratic sort of man.
It is plain, he said.
To begin with, are they not free? And is not the city chock-full of liberty and freedom of speech? And has not every man license to do as he likes?
So it is said, he replied.
And where there is such license, it is obvious that everyone would arrange a plan for leading his own life in the way that pleases him. Obvious.
All sorts and conditions of men, then would arise in this polity more than in any other?
Of course.
Possibly, said I, this is the most beautiful of polities, as a garment of many colors, embroidered with all kinds of hues, so this, decked and diversified with every type of character, would appear the most beautiful. And perhaps many would judge it to be the most beautiful, like boys and women when they see bright-colored things.
Yes indeed, he said.
Yes, said I, and it is the fit place, my good friend, in which to look for a constitution.
Why so?
Because, owing to this license, it includes all kinds, and it seems likely that anyone who wishes to organize a state, as we were just now

doing, must find his way to a democratic city and select the model that please him, as if in a bazaar of constitutions, and after making his choice, establish his own.[24]

Of course, the Greek city-state cannot serve as a model for an advanced industrial society, nor can the elitist attitude which led Plato to reject the democratic society as the preferable form of society be accepted. However, his description of how life is lived in a democracy is still relevant today. For it is in democracy that specialness of individuals and communities is developed.

The question of the quality of life in the advanced industrial countries of the twentieth century has been discussed in many philosophical schools. It has been widely recognized that technological advancement does not necessarily bring a better life, although an increasingly efficient productive system is a prerequisite for a life of real quality. The existentialists have shown that the blind acceptance of scientific advancement leads to a nonauthentic life. The American pragmatists, even while they argued for an extension of the scientific method, recognized that in the end there are certain vital questions in man's life which cannot be solved by technological and scientific advancement.

Today's widespread doubt concerning the effects of industrialization is in sharp contrast to the prevalent attitude in the nineteenth century, when it was generally assumed that it would be foolish to stand in the way of "progress." Even the most brutal forms of exploitation were excused because they contributed to an advancement of society's productive capacities.

The new democrats, in their emphasis on the quality of life, are expressing in practice the sense of uneasiness which has found theoretical expression in the past. As they have become involved in political action, they have come to realize that the basic problem is that institutions do not exist which enable men to exercise real control over their lives. They do not accept the assumption that suffering is necessary for human progress, but point out that the material affluence which has been praised so highly has been achieved through the suffering and sacrifice of the working class. Those who have worked are the ones who have the rightful claim to a life worth living, and they are the ones who must have the power to make decisions governing their lives.

The new democratic theory emphasizes that the quality of man's everyday life, the life of man as a working being, is the primary concern. Science and an understanding of general laws can be important, but a distinction between science and everyday life is necessary so that qualitative criteria can be applied to the so-called advances in societal development. Science and technology are not enemies of man, but neither can they claim to be the final test and judge of what kind of life is fit to live.

Science is properly understood as a reconstruction of certain aspects of our experience. A good scientific model is useful when it provides an understanding of the character of the general laws of nature and of tendencies present in society. As long as one is interested in prediction, that is in the results in the narrowest sense, a scientific model can be assumed to properly portray reality. A problem arises, however, when it is claimed that all reality, including man's everyday life, should be dominated by abstractions which are judged only in terms of their ability to make accurate predictions.

An adequate philosophical position must consider all areas of human experience. It is not by accident that the liberal democrats and dialectical materialists have failed to develop an adequate aesthetics because they focus on a limited part of

141

man's experience. Aesthetics, which considers a realm of experience different from that considered by science, is concerned with human products that portray the special characteristics of human life. In science we look for a general law under which all experience can be subsumed, while in the sphere studied by aesthetics we look for descriptions of the special experiences or the individual moments in life which are heightened to form a new kind of experience. Quality, rather than quantity, is the test used in aesthetics. Any philosophy which is to be adequate to man's total experience must include the possibility for the development of an aesthetic theory. The poverty of life in the industrialized nations, even the life of those who are materially wealthy, is one of the chief indications that the traditional theories have failed.

The development of a rich scientific and artistic life is necessary for there to be a life of high quality. The abstraction process which takes place in the creation of a scientific theory or a work of art is necessary to increase both the efficiency of human productivity and human awareness of the life we live. Science and art help us understand where we are at present and where we are going so that we may be in a position of controlling our existence. In the sense that democracy is essentially the state of controllable activity, science and aesthetics play a crucial role in the democratic life. Indeed, a democratic society is one in which science and art together can be developed to the fullest.

Abstractions from the concrete, such as a work of art or a scientific theory, are necessary if we are to understand the concrete and to formulate alternate ways of living. The problem arises only when a particular theory or way of understanding is mistaken for reality itself. Thus, for example, the "scientific" method has often been claimed to be the only correct way of comprehending life, which means that aesthetics, ethics, and other areas which understand man's life and culture are dismissed or relegated to mere personal opinion. The "scientism" of the liberal democrats and the dialectical materialists has been an important factor in preventing them from developing an adequate theory of society.

Science and art are but two of the ways in which man comes to understand and experience his everyday life. Through experiences of artistic and scientific work, man comprehends, but he does not exhaust the content of his daily life. The concrete, the sphere from which theoretical activity abstracts, is, as Marx put it, "concrete because it is a bringing together of many determinations, that is, it is a unity in diversity."[25] The community is the concrete social unit of man's life—it is not an abstraction from his work and life but is the concrete life of man as it is actually lived and experienced. Our daily life in community is a radical mixture of all kinds of desires, hopes, and dreams. We live and work in community. Here we spend our time; we love, we hate, and we desire. Our life is full of contradictions, in the sense that a plurality of intentions exists, and these contradictions must be worked through within the life of the community. In the working process, what is not yet present is seen as a real possibility, and the past is experienced as a real part of our lives. Man's experience is historical; his past experiences confront him in the form of human products; through interaction with them he re-creates his world.

An understanding of the life of man, whether it comes through a new painting, a new physical theory, or a new form of government, influences and changes the character of human reality. These products of man become a part of the unity of diversity which makes up the life which we live.

In our everyday life we answer to the situation in which we find ourselves. Our life is not the creation of the mind or of

143

daring decisions, as some existentialists would want us believe, but it is the result of our working with the world in which we live. Man, in his most concrete life, is a responsive being, and he develops in response to the world.

The test of the quality of life is the extent to which people can realize their potentialities within a community. The purpose of understanding man's life is to promote and develop the community. The advanced industrial societies have built their riches by alienating the individual from his working process and his community and by robbing him of his specialness. To create a democracy today means that communities must be created which are based on the activity of man as a working being. In a democracy interaction between man and nature and among men is encouraged. This is the basis for social development. The community is based on work as the creative process in which men engage.

The realization of one's potentiality and the preservation of specialness is possible only in communities controlled by those who live and work in them. Control is not an end in itself, but it is a means by which a life of real quality can be created. The new democratic theory, which understands democracy as control of working and living situations, is raising the question of the quality of life in the political and social realm. In order to create a social life of quality, it is necessary to develop a revolutionary movement which brings about a society under the control of those living and working in society.

The control of the environment through community life must, of course, be a form of social control. Democracy is not primarily a form of government, nor even a way of making decisions; it is a way of living. As a form of life, democracy is not utopia—it is not an ideal state toward which we must strive—but it is the movement present in the world creating a new form of life. In an attempt to describe the state of flux, based on praxis, which is present in a genuine democracy some have described it as a state of permanent revolution. To correctly understand democracy as community, and not as a particular form of government or way of decision making, does not bring democracy into being, but it does focus our attention on the problem of the quality of man's life.

When the question of the purpose and nature of production is raised, new kinds of concepts to discuss the nature of society must be developed. The question of how production can be increased is primarily a technical question. A technician can tell us what we must do to achieve certain results, and the changes which a technician requires are applicable to many different productive processes. A technician's advice may be used to produce tanks or cars, toothpaste or napalm. When Americans speak of the sciences being value free, they generally mean that the technical and applied sciences can be utilized for any kind of production.

To ask the question, How ought we to live? is to raise an ethical issue which is blurred or dismissed as long as we are primarily concerned with the quantity of production. To develop a society in which not only *many* objects can be produced, but many *good* objects, requires both the optimalization and the humanization of society.

As discussed previously, in the United States a large apparatus has been created which has no function except to sell what is produced. The productive process is determined by the possibility for selling products in a commodity-oriented society. At the same time, in the socialist countries the productive process is determined by a massive bureaucracy. Both systems would be more efficient if it were possible to bring production under the control of the communities so that the exterior motivation for production could be eliminated. Only if the quality of products can be seriously questioned can a really efficient society be created in the advanced industrial countries.

The theory of the new democrats presupposes a fundamental change in the productive process, and until this new form of production has been created, the new democrats will remain revolutionaries in the societies in which they live. Participation in the revolutionary movement requires turning away from individual escape from the new kinds of poverty found in the advanced industrialized societies. It also requires that the oppressive nature of the current order be recognized and that democracy be understood as community control in which maximum specialness of groups and individuals can be developed. The revolutionary movement for a new society is only beginning to be formed, but we can already see that democracy is properly understood as the state in which man controls his fate—a state in which the concrete life, the community, is realized.

The new democratic theory has validity insofar as there are groups which have a real interest in forming a revolutionary movement. The basis for a substantial democratization does not lie in local desires for more independence, but in an international movement expressing the real tendencies present in our world, which will lead to a democratic social order. While the new democratic theory will remain incomplete until the theory and practice of the various elements of the movement are taken into consideration, the fact that a genuinely new theory is developing today and that there is a real possibility for a new kind of democratic movement is in no way lessened. The revolt against the order which was established after World War II has already begun, and it will continue. The question is not whether we will have a new theory and a new society, but what form the new society will take. We are in the normal position of any relevant theoretical work: whether or not we think about what we do, a new era is emerging, in which radically new forms of social and political life are present. As Marx said, "We do it, but do not know what we do." The problem, which requires a genuine unity of theory and practice, is to develop the new democratic society.

The task of the new democrats is to work for the development of a revolutionary movement. Reforms are necessary and possible today, but unless they take place through the activity of the revolutionary democratic coalition, no qualitative change in society will take place. An organization which can unite the various forces having an interest in a new kind of democracy is becoming more and more necessary. The development of a revolutionary movement and the careful consideration of the form this movement will take is the most important prerequisite for a new democratic society. A new kind of society fit to live in can be thought of today, not as an abstract wish, but as a concrete possibility.

References

GOODMAN, PAUL, *People or Personnel and Like a Conquered Province*, Random House, New York, 1968.

> The latest collection of essays by Paul Goodman. Goodman presents numerous suggestions for changes which could improve the quality of life and serve to develop communities. While his suggestions are utopian and are not based on an analysis of the forces working for change, they still show that a really new style of life is possible in an industrialized nation.

HINTON, WILLIAM, *Fanshen. A Documentary of Revolution in a Chinese Village*, Random House, New York, 1968.

> It is difficult for us to realize that qualitative changes really *do* take place in society. *Fanshen* is a study of a revolutionary change and the

way in which a really new style of life was created by a successful revolution. This book has been important to many people in the movement as an example of what a revolutionary change in society involves.

LONG PRISCILLA (ed.), *The New Left. A Collection of Essays*, Porter Sargent, Boston, 1969.

> A collection of essays on the New Left. Perhaps one of the best books showing the theoretical development of the New Left and the kind of program being articulated. Included is a short statement by a group of twenty-five people from many different fields that there are three revolutions underway: cybernation revolution, the weaponry revolution, and the human rights revolution (The Triple Revolution). Although no class analysis is given in this statement, it does indicate the wide-ranging changes taking place which make a true democracy possible. Democracy is defined as "a community of men and women who are able to understand, express and determine their lives as dignified human beings."

MANUEL, FRANK E. (ed.), *Utopias and Utopian Thought*, Beacon Press, Boston, 1965.

> A collection of contemporary discussions of utopia. Many of these consider the creation of communities, which is one of the traditional parts of a utopian theory.

ROSZAK, THEODORE, *The Making of a Counter Culture*, Doubleday, New York, 1969.

> A discussion of the new culture being created by the youth of America. A good theoretical discussion which shows the revolt against the meaninglessness of the life inherited by the middle class.

WOLFF, ROBERT PAUL, *The Poverty of Liberalism*, Beacon Press, Boston, 1968.

> A philosophical criticism of the liberal theory. The final chapter discusses the concept of community and its importance for building an alternative theory of democracy.

10
Building a Revolutionary Movement

Until now the philosophers have only interpreted the world in various ways. The point, however, is to change it.
MARX

The primary question of contemporary democratic theory is, in the end, the question of the proper organization of the revolutionary movement. In this chapter we shall consider what it means for a movement to be revolutionary, and we shall propose a possible strategy for a successful revolutionary movement in an advanced industrialized nation.

In our previous discussions we have seen that the revolutionary movement is based on three forces in the industrialized nations of the world: the workers (all those who have no property but their labor time); those excluded from the benefits of current social and economic life; and those who understand that the democratic society is in their interest. These three forces have an interest in bringing bureaucrats under control, in overcoming alienation, and in creating genuine communities. Since the new democratic order can be created only by a fundamental economic and social change, the discussion of the new democratic theory must close, as it began, with a consideration of the contemporary revolutionary movement which makes a democratic order possible today.

A revolution is a fundamental change in the quality of life; that is, it is a change in the relationship of man to his working situation. Put in more classical terms, a revolution is a change in the ruling classes. Revolution is not a coup d'état, a simple change of government; it is not an election in which one party substitutes itself for another, but it is a transfer of control over the means of production from one class to another. In the twentieth century, the democratic revolutionary movement works for the creation of a system in which the means of production are put under the control of the workers, who are organized around the communities in which they live and work.

A revolutionary transformation does not take place in a predetermined way; what is important is that there be a transfer of control over the means of production. Changes in government, which do not necessarily bring about a revolutionary change, take place in many forms: through elections, by a quick seizure of power, and by prolonged civil wars. Revolutionary transformations, as well, come about in many different ways, depending upon the situation. A revolution requires a fundamental change in the class structure. Political activity is, of course, also an important part of a movement seeking revolutionary change. The new democrats have developed their revolutionary position over a period of years, as they have come to understand that the problem is to bring the working situation under the control of the workers.

A movement is held together by common experiences and common loyalties. It exists as a *local* organization. The democratic theory which has been discussed here has been the product of many local movements reacting to particular situations in similar ways. The movement is neither governed by the majority nor is it organized in the pattern of democratic centralism developed by Stalin. The democratic movement, as it has become revolutionary in character, has begun to seek fundamental social change. A revolutionary movement is not a pressure group organized around specific issues to improve the existing order, but is a thoughtful and coordinated response to a repressive social system.

The primary task of the revolutionary movement now is to sustain itself and to assess realistically the possibility for revolution in the industrialized nations. As a movement which is just beginning, but which is based on the objective forces in society having an interest in fundamental social change, the democratic movement is going beyond disruption and is organizing as a force which can seize power.

Democracy is the only form of society in which man can develop fully. This fact, which is at the basis of the revolutionary activity, will remain true even if the revolutionary movement is not immediately successful. Democracy is a live option today in a radically new way, and it is necessary for everyone, whether he is conscious of the fact or not, to participate in choosing the future course of society. We are all, whether we like it or not, either part of the problem or part of the solution.

The heart of a Marxist theory of history is the basic understanding that there are genuinely different possibilities for historical development. Through revolutionary praxis new alternatives are developed. Even though it is correct to claim that democracy is necessary today, one need not be committed to a strict historical determinism. The revolutionary movement, if it is to be successful, must realize that its demands can be thwarted in many ways and that success will come only if a proper analysis and strategy can be developed.

In social reality we are presented with alternatives given to us by historical development, and we must choose which path to take. Even to refrain from choosing means that we have assented to live in the society as it is currently constituted. In order to develop a revolutionary movement it is necessary to consider alternatives which are available at each stage of development and to operate effectively within the situation presented to us. We live in a world not of our choosing. This world, however, is a product of human activity and is constantly re-created by our choices. It is this fundamental awareness of man's basic role as a being who is determined by history, but who can also make history, that is at the heart of the revolutionary movement today.

The two major democratic theories, liberal democracy and dialectical materialism, have both denied this view of history and political action. The liberals have insisted that it is not necessary to choose a particular economic form. For the liberal, society is nothing more than a framework, a rule of law, which provides the conditions that enable individuals to create their own lives. But this freedom of the liberal is abstract. The liberal theory does permit revolutionary change as an alternative. It claims to be a democratic theory of government, not of society, and leaves the crucial area of the relationship of the worker to his means of production beyond social control. Despite the fact that the pluralistic, liberal view of democracy claims not to require a choice of social system, it permits only a capitalist or a social democratic system to exist. No serious challenge to the existing economic and social order is permitted. In a liberal society, one must live by the rules of the game, and these rules claim to give individual freedom. The problem comes, however, when the rules themselves are called into question. The liberal theory, while claiming to be the basis for any free society, prohibits the development of a social movement for revolutionary change.

The dialectical materialists have also argued that no choice is possible in history, but they have done this on the basis of the conception that history is a determined order. It is claimed that we are driven by forces beyond the control of the individual and, it would seem, beyond the power of any revolutionary movement. According to that view, a revolutionary social movement which really changes the world cannot exist.

The argument between the liberal democrats and the dialectical materialists concerning the nature of historical development is one form of the traditional philosophical argument between the advocates of free will and determinism. As in so many other cases the arguments of the liberal democrats and the dialectical materialists depend upon each other for their existence. In the end both positions support the current social order by denying the possibility for creating a movement to develop another kind of world. The result is that both the liberal democratic and dialectical materialistic theories become more and more a formality and an ideology which support the status quo, while allowing less and less real control over life. Both deny the basic proposition of the new democratic theory that man lives in a world he did not choose but that is being created by his choices.

If the new democrats are to be successful, they cannot afford to repeat the mistakes of the liberal democrats and dialectical materialists, who consistently underestimated the capability of the "other side" to solve its own problems. After World War II, partly because they were hampered by an insufficient view of historical development and knowledge of their opponents, both sides confidently expected that their opponents would collapse. However, this was not the case, and instead the two sides have emerged as allies in opposition to democratic forces within their own societies.

After World War II the liberal democrats were certain that the communist order was unstable, and they expected the people of Central Europe to free themselves from "communist domination." Economic and political problems in Central and Eastern Europe were so great that it appeared that no stable political order could be established on the basis of the Red Army. However, instead of the expected rollback of the communists, the socialist societies have stabilized themselves. It is now certain that they will not voluntarily be replaced by a liberal democratic order. Socialism and a socialist form of society are firmly entrenched in Central Europe, and a viable economic and social order has been established.

The disappointment of the liberals, who expected that communism would soon prove to be an unstable form of society which would give way to a liberal "western" democracy, was matched by the disappointment of the dialectical materialists, who waited in vain for a victory of communism in Western Europe and other parts of the capitalist world. Like the liberals, the dialectical materialists had faith that the people would see that *their* system was better. According to their analysis, capitalism was full of contradictions and would not be able to solve its economic and political problems. Capitalism, however, proved to be not nearly so unstable as its enemies had thought. Instead of victory of the "masses" over the capitalists, the masses appeared to become more and more a part of the bourgeois social order.

One possibility for social development today is that the process of self-correction will continue and that democracy will become a more and more meaningless slogan in both East and West. Instead of striking back at the new democrats, the system will attempt to bring them within itself, to offer individual personal advancement while refusing to bring about the fundamental social change which is demanded. By offering the individual a personal life of comfort, to be paid for by his withdrawal from social and political activity, the current order can "solve" many of its current problems, at least in the short run. As in the past the most obvious and annoying difficulties can be overcome by minimal change within the system. Of course in order to do this, democracy as a theoretically and practically valuable form of society must be abandoned. The price for stability will be the abandonment of all pretence at being democratic, but for those in authority this price does not always seem too high.

Perhaps this alternative for social development can be best understood by taking two examples from the groups which can form a part of a revolutionary movement: the blacks in the United States and the intellectuals in Eastern Europe. The process of assimilation of these two groups has already begun, and if it is successful, it will be difficult to develop a genuinely democratic movement. Richard Nixon, who would hardly be on anyone's list of radicals, has perhaps most clearly stated the ideology of those who look for an integration of the blacks into the existing social order. His program could just as well be put forward by Lyndon Johnson or any of the other liberal democrats. Nixon has proposed that the "positive" side of the black power argument be accepted and has attempted to use the terminology of black power to integrate the blacks into the existing capitalistic system. Black power, for Nixon, means that private funds, private energies, and private talents are enlisted to give incentives to private industry in order to solve the problems of poverty. His answer to the challenge of the blacks is to use the doctrines of free enterprise or, as he puts it, to give the Negro an equal chance at the starting line.

Of course any analysis by a new democrat would quickly point out that the same doctrines of free enterprise which supposedly made America successful are those which required the blacks in the United States to live in slavery for more than three hundred years. By giving all blacks an equal chance at the starting line (which assumes that they will not be equal shortly thereafter), the hope for individual advancement and a way out of the oppression can be created, which may temporarily thwart the development of a revolutionary social movement.

If black power is transformed into black capitalism and black cultural nationalism, no economic change will take place. The blacks will be integrated into the capitalist system, and the alienation and manipulation present in society will increase. The black communities will be destroyed, and the blacks will have no alternative but to become part of a white society if they are to survive. Failure to succeed will continue to be attributed to an individual lack of certain abilities, and the social root of alienation will be ignored. The attempt at integration in the United States is most clearly seen in the call for black capitalism and in the creation of a poverty program which is aimed at preventing the formation of a movement for fundamental social change.

Just as the problem of the blacks in the United States can be temporarily solved by giving hope for individual advancement within the current order, so the problem of the dissatisfied intellectuals in Central Europe can be solved by allowing the possibility for "freedom." Of course the crucial point is that the possibility for individual advancement requires a renunciation of participation in a movement which seeks a fundamental change in society. By providing money and material goods, it is hoped that the growing social movement can be stopped.

The most obvious strategy for those in authority will be to attempt to integrate the dissidents into society. Part of this

156

strategy is an effort to channel the creative energies of individuals presently working within the revolutionary movement into projects which try to solve problems that threaten the stability of the system. The optimalization achieved by integration will not, however, be accompanied by the development of social institutions in which workers will control the means of production. Alienation and isolation will increase and take on new forms. The destruction of communities, by providing hope for individual release from intolerable conditions, will be furthered. There will be an increasing number of people excluded from society because they do not run the race well in accordance with the established rules. Such a solution will leave unaltered the social and economic conditions, which will produce new material for a revolutionary movement. To integrate is really to choose to do nothing about the basic problems of bureaucracy, of alienation, and of the quality of life, which are at the center of the new democratic theory. But it is an open alternative, and a movement which is working for genuine change in society must recognize that much of the current unrest might be temporarily dampened by integration.

If integration is successful, the traditional strategy for building a revolutionary movement will not work. Past revolutionary movements have been mobilized on a mass basis with the aid of open opposition from the ruling authorities. The current movement has been helped enormously by the use of police in many countries to break up peaceful demonstrations. To an outsider it sometimes appears that the movement has only one common program—opposition to police brutality. No matter what country one may examine, the police, as the organized force of the state, are the subject of attack. Police brutality against those seeking justifiable changes has been one of the greatest mobilizing forces for the movement.

Building a Revolutionary Movement

In the past, the presence of open oppression has forced the movement to create vanguard struggles. Particularly in under-developed and exceptionally oppressive societies, such as pre-revolutionary Russia and China, it was possible for a disciplined revolutionary movement to seize power. In the advanced industrialized nations, however, it does not appear that the strategy of basing a revolutionary movement upon the opposition from the state will be successful. The small, well-organized parties which have led to the revolution in other countries do not appear to be the proper organizational form for the revolutionary movement in advanced industrialized countries.

One of the surest ways for a disciplined movement to be built would be for those in power to adopt openly oppressive measures in order to suppress those who are attacking the current order of society. If this is done, opposition to the system will increase, as the use of force will create a growing number of revolutionaries. The demarcation between those seeking fundamental change and those asking for reform will become clear, and a bloody and forceful battle can be expected.

Traditional revolutionary theory has assumed that those in authority will not tolerate the existence of a revolutionary movement and will react with force against it. However, in the liberal democracies, and to an increasing extent in the socialist countries, those in power have learned that it is more effective to promote revolutionaries on an individual basis within the system than to fight against them as an organized movement. During the early days of the rebellion in the black communities, young rioters were supplied with symbols of authority and were given an individual chance for advancement within the existing police organization. The colleges and universities in the United States have promoted and furthered individual radicals in the hope that they will settle down when they are given responsibility. Of course the assumption is that any individual who accepts the promotion within the existing order will stop being revolutionary and will lend his talents to the preservation of the existing system.

If the revolutionary movement is to be successful, it must recognize that a combination of integration and oppression will be used by those now in authority in their attempts to break up the movement. In both the East and the West the opportunity for personal advancement for all who are willing to integrate themselves into the system is held open. Attempts are made not to close off access to any potential members of the revolutionary movement who are willing to seek personal advancement rather than revolutionary change. On the other hand, oppression is becoming more and more open against those who maintain and develop a revolutionary position. In Czechoslovakia the oppression found its most open form in the invasion by troops from the Soviet Union and some other members of the Warsaw Pact. This invasion did not result in massive arrests, but instead steady pressure was applied on those seeking change, while the possibilities for personal accommodation were held open. In the United States and Western Europe the oppression of members of the revolutionary movement has been steadily growing. This oppression is aimed primarily at individuals who become particularly outspoken, but a way out is held open to those who are willing to participate in society.

Such a two-pronged attack on the movement is difficult, but it is also the most effective. Unfortunately, for those in power it is difficult to limit the oppression and to identify clearly those who will integrate themselves into the system if they are given sufficient opportunity. Every time that there is an open attack on the members of the revolutionary movement, new people are convinced that the system does, indeed, rest upon force and that only a fundamental change in the groups which control the means of production will bring about a democratic order.

The revolutionary movement, if it is to be successful, must reckon with the dual approach of those in power and must be aware of the contradiction present in that approach. So long as they are not required to act in a counterrevolutionary manner, the members of the movement can openly accept positions within society. Oppression, when it comes, should be obvious and clear to all who have an interest in fundamental social change. The guerrilla strategy of participation in society while opposing the social order is becoming applicable in the advanced industrialized countries, just as it is now being used in the developing countries. The guerrilla in the advanced industrialized countries must be part of a movement. He must also seek to create an environment which permits him to live and work in society while taking part in the revolutionary movement. The guerrilla strategy is not a romantic dream, but is a necessity dictated by the dual threats of integration and repression being used by those in authority.

To base a movement on the assumption that the opposition will fight back is to leave the initiative to the authorities, to lose control of the movement, and to place its fate in the hands of those in power. Of course, in some situations where openly oppressive measures are used, the opposition to the existing order will be built by those in power, but provocation of the oppressive forces cannot be the primary strategy for developing a movement based on the real interests of the people. To build a movement today requires organizing revolutionary forces within existing institutions. Those seeking change in an advanced society should be engaged in the productive process. They should accept positions within the existing order while maintaining their organized opposition to the system and not merely to certain of its symptoms. The movement must be composed of those who are engaged in production and who nevertheless feel themselves to be part of the movement in opposition to the present form of society. Organizations of revolutionaries, which cut across traditional class and union boundaries, are necessary to unite those in opposition to authority.

The goal of the movement must be no less than a revolutionary transformation of society. Economic and social institutions must be brought under the control of the workers, and new communities must be created. The strategy which appears most likely to succeed is the takeover of society through a guerrilla movement within the society.

The practical problem becomes, of course, how we can tell the difference between actual revolutionary reform and mere meeting on the surface of revolutionary demands by the existing authority. How can we tell whether a revolutionary movement has succeeded in changing society and has itself not merely been integrated into the existing society? If we are clear as to the nature of the democratic society, then it is possible to judge whether or not reforms are really revolutionary. The most fundamental question which must be asked whenever any reform is proposed is, Who exercises control over the institution? A reform can be accepted only if it works in the direction of giving the workers, as workers, the control over their institutions. We must ask, What forms of alienation are present in the proposed reforms? Only if alienation is decreased, that is, if it is possible for man to increase the control over his own life both in the working process and in his free time, is it a genuinely revolutionary reform. Finally, we must ask, What is the relationship to other groups under the reform? Only if communities are developed in which the specialness of individuals and of the community can be developed can the reform be called revolutionary. The movement can be successful if it can mobilize the forces in opposition to the existing order and bring about a revolutionary transformation of the advanced industrial societies. The choice between revolutionary reform and merely accepting the basic order of society is not arbitrary. It is a choice which involves the very nature and quality of human life and experience.

The movement for fundamental reform is just beginning. The democratic forces are finding their way together, and a genuinely revolutionary and international movement exists in the world. This movement is international because many people, whether in the East or the West, are discovering that they have adopted similar programs and have reacted in similar ways to what first appeared to be local problems. The problems are not local in origin, and because they are not, we can now speak meaningfully of a new democratic theory and a new democratic movement. In order to be successful, it is necessary for the new democrats to see themselves at the beginning of a movement which *must* succeed if a genuinely humane society is to be created. The new democrats are guerrillas within the current order and can use their talents and training to further the creation of a society which is under the control of the workers.

The movement now, at the beginning of its revolutionary phase, is faced with the problem of a proper organization. How can a revolutionary movement exist in an advanced industrialized country? What kind of discipline is necessary for members of the movement? How much centralization is needed? What is the proper relationship of the members of the movement to the leaders? All of these questions are being seriously discussed in the movement. How they will be answered will depend upon the theory and practice of the movement as it develops. Organization becomes the crucial theoretical question once it is understood that the current order is producing its own contradictions and there is a concrete possibility for a new order. Past Marxist discussion, particularly before Stalinism came to be accepted as the only orthodox Marxist formulation, also centered on the question of proper organization. This question will be the focus for the important and creative works of the near future both in theory and in practice.

The response of the movement will depend upon the situation and the special interests of those involved. In black America the language and organizational form of armed revolution are becoming increasingly relevant. On the other hand, it would be naïve for white America to speak of an armed revolution, when it is white America which is oppressing the blacks and is waging a war of aggression in many parts of the world. But white Americans can realize that until they free themselves, their government will continue to engage in wars of aggression and will continue to destroy the black community. In Central Europe, where a form of socialism has already been achieved, the situation will require a different approach. There the democratic movement can work within the authentic Marxist tradition.

The particular response of the movement, because it is local in character, will depend upon the special situation in which it is found. Accordingly, the new theory articulated here will be altered as a genuinely international movement is created which includes all the oppressed peoples of the world. But there is a common theory uniting the movement, and it makes cooperation possible among the various groups in the world which have an interest in fundamental social change.

For now, we can sum up: A new era of history has begun, and a new movement to radically change the world is a reality.

163

Building a Revolutionary Movement

The new democratic theory is an articulation of this force. The theory is only beginning to be worked out, but it is already a reality. Hope for a genuinely democratic social order depends upon the success of the movement now being built.

References

The references listed in previous chapters consist mainly of books relevant to the revolutionary movement. However, several publications carry on the discussions concerning the nature and future of the revolutionary movement. They serve as the best source of information for understanding the issues. Several of these current publications, with their addresses, are listed below.

Black Panther, Box 2967, Custom House, San Francisco, Calif., 94126.
> The weekly newspaper of the Black Panther Party.

Guardian, 32 W.22nd Street, New York, N.Y., 10009.
> An independent radical news weekly. One of the best sources of current news of the movement.

Leviathan, 250 Mullen Avenue, San Francisco, Calif., 94110.
> A monthly movement magazine of political opinion and analysis.

Movement, 55 Colton Street, San Francisco, Calif., 94603
> A monthly movement newspaper of news and analysis.

New England Free Press, 791 Tremont Street, Boston, Mass., 02118.
> A good source for radical books and pamphlets on all of the major issues under discussion in the movement.

New University Conference, 622 Diversey Parkway, rm 403a, Chicago, Illinois, 60614.
> New University Conference is a national organization of radicals who work in, around and in spite of institutions of higher education. They publish a bi-monthly newsletter, plus occasional pamphlets.

164

References

Progressive Labor, G.P.O. Box 808, Brooklyn, N.Y., 11201.
   The national bimonthly periodical of the Progressive Labor Party.

Radical America, 1237 Spaight Street, Madison, Wisconsin, 53703.
   A journal published ten times per year which is devoted to theoretical discussions of current issues in the movement.

Radical Education Project, Box 561a, Detroit, Mich., 48232.
   Pamphlets and other information can be obtained from REP, which was originally started as the research and literature distribution arm of Students for a Democratic Society.

Ramparts, 495 Beach Street, San Francisco, Calif.
   The only nationally important movement publication with a "slick" format.

Revolutionary Youth Movement, Box 5421, Station E, Atlanta, Georgia, 30307.
   The paper of the organization formed out of the dissolution of SDS in the summer of 1969. *RYM* includes many of the leaders of SDS during 1969 and is seeking to build a resolutionary youth movement on principles such as the repudiation of white skin privilege and of male chauvinism.

Socialist Revolution, 1445 Stockton Street, San Francisco, California, 94133.
   A theoretical journal published bi-monthly which seeks to lay the basis for a revolutionary socialist movement.

Women's Liberation, Radical Feminism, P.O. Box AA, Old Chelsea Station, New York, 10011.
   An annual collection of articles by leaders of the women's liberation movement.

Three good bibliographies are

APTHEKER, BETTINA, *Higher Education and the Student Rebellion in the United States. 1960–1969.* Bibliographical Series no. 6, American Institute of Marxist Studies, 20 East 30th Street, New York, N.Y., 10016.

CISLER, CINDY, *Women: A Bibliography*. May be ordered from 102 West 80th Street, New York, New York, 10024.
The most complete available bibliography on the women's question.

KAISER, ERNEST, "Recent Literature on Black Liberation Struggles and the Ghetto Crisis (A Bibliographical Survey)," *Science and Society*, Spring, 1969, vol. XXXIII, pp. 168–196.

Notes

CHAPTER 1

1. Dialectical materialism is used throughout this book to refer to the official theoretical position developed in the Soviet Union. In Chapters 3 and 4 we shall discuss the nature of authentic Marxism and dialectical materialism more explicitly.

CHAPTER 2

2. After the local elections of 1969, there was one black mayor out of 270, one black legislator out of 174, no black sheriffs, and no black statewide officials in Mississippi.
3. Robert A. Dahl, *Preface to Democratic Theory*, University of Chicago, 1956, p. 131.
4. *Ibid.*, p. 152.

CHAPTER 3

5. These two are Antonio Gramsci, "Critical Notes on an Attempt at a Popular Presentation of Marxism by Bukharin" in *The Modern Prince and Other Writings*, International Publishers, New York, 1957; and Georg Lukacs, "N. Bukharin: Theorie des historischen Materialismus," *Werke*, vol. II, Luchterhand, Neuwied, Germany, 1968, pp. 598–611.
6. Eduard Bernstein, *Evolutionary Socialism*, Schocken, New York, 1961, p. 149.
7. *Ibid.*, p. 154.

CHAPTER 4

8. Georg Lukacs, *Werke*, vol. II, Luchterhand, Neuwied, Germany, 1968, p. 171. All translations are my own unless otherwise indicated.

9. Georg Lukacs, *Schriften zur Ideologie und Politik*, edited byLudz, Luchterhand, Neuwied, Germany, 1967, p. 328.

10. *Ibid.*, p. 599.

11. *Ibid.*, p. 704.

12. *Ibid.*, p. 674.

13. *Ibid.*, p. 689.

14. Georg Lukacs, "Interview: At Home with György Lukacs," as reprinted in English in *The New Hungarian Quarterly*, Spring, 1968, p. 78.

15. Karl Marx, "Thesis on Feuerbach," no. 3, as translated in *Writings of the Young Marx on Philosophy and Society*, edited by Easton and Guddat, Doubleday, New York, 1967, p. 401.

16. Karl Marx, *The Eighteenth Brumaire of Louis Bonaparte*, International Publishers, New York, 1963, p. 15.

17. Karl Marx, *Capital*, vol. I, International Publishers, New York, 1967, p. 177.

18. Lukacs, "Interview: At Home with György Lucacs," *op. cit.* p. 75.

CHAPTER 7

19. William W. Boyer, *Bureaucracy on Trial*, University of Indiana, Indianapolis, Ind. 1964, pp. 167–168.

20. Lenin, "State and Revolution," in *Selected Works*, vol. II, International Publishers, New York, 1967, p. 345.

CHAPTER 8

21. Two good translations of Marx's early writings are *Karl Marx: Early Writings*, translated and edited by T. B. Bottomore, McGraw-Hill, New York, 1964; and *Writings of the Young Marx on Philosophy and Society*, edited and translated by Easton and Guddat, Doubleday, New York, 1967.

22. Karl Marx, *Theorien über den Mehrwert*, Teil 2, Dietz, Berlin, 1959, p. 107. My translation.

CHAPTER 9

23. Mihaly Vajda, "Entfremdung und Sozialismus: Diskussion Ungarischer Marxisten," *Praxis*, vol. III, no. 4, 1967, pp. 556–563.
24. Plato, *Republic*, vol. VIII, p. 557. Paul Shorey's translation in *Plato : The Collected Dialogues*, edited by Edith Hamilton, Pantheon, New York, 1963.
25. Karl Marx, *Grundrisse der Kritik der Politischen Okonomie*, Dietz. Berlin, 1953, p. 21. My translation.

Index

Index

China, 158
CIA (Central Intelligence
  Agency), 23
Civil rights movement, 16-17
  failure of liberal democratic
  theory and, 16-20
Coercion, bureaucracy and, 100,
  129
Cold war, 1-10
Commodity exchange, 126
Communism, 154
  Marx's theory of, 40
  See also Marx, Karl; Marxism
Communist Party, 93, 104
Community, 86
  society based upon, 137-38,
  143-44
Community control, 18-19, 146
Consumer society, 127-29
Control of everyday life, 135-47
Control of means of production,
  94-95
Cooperation, society in terms of,
  83-84
Cooperatives, 86
Cooptation of the revolution,
  156-59
Cultural nationalism, black, 156
Cultural poverty, 75
Czechoslovakia, 42-43, 93, 159

Dahl, Robert A., 27
Decentralization, 102-03, 108, 110
Decision-making, 102, 108
Declaration of Independence, 91
Democracy
  communism as true form of, 40
  revolutionary movement and,
  151
Democratic centralism, 43

Democratic coalition, reshaping
  of, 65-79
  blacks as part of, 74-75, 77
  intellectuals, 70-72
  revolutionary potential of poor,
  67-69, 71, 74-75
  workers, 69-70, 72-73
Democratic Convention (Chicago,
  1968), 21-22
Democratic Marxism, 33-45
  party revolutionary praxis,
  40-45
  power politics, 38-39
  return to, 33-34, 39-40, 45
  Soviet formulation of dialectical
  materialism, 34-37
  See also Lukacs, Georg
Democratic Party, 70
Democratic socialism, 42-43, 93-94
Democratic theory, see Liberal
  democratic theory
Development of capitalism, 68-72
Dialectical materialism, 5, 55,
  153-54
  Soviet formulation of, 34-37
Domination, end of, 78-79
Dropouts, 125

East-West relations, 1-11
  cold war, 2, 3-5
  new democratic theory, 7-11
  peaceful coexistence, 2, 5-6
  technocratic, 2, 6-7
"Economic and Philosophic
  Manuscripts" (Marx), 120
Education, role in society of,
  76-77, 111, 115-16
Election process, 25-27
England, 10, 70
Engels, Friedrich, 88

172

Index

Index

majority rule and minority
rights, 23-24, 28
superiority of Marxist viewpoint,
40
war in Viet Nam, 20-23
Liberal experimentation, 60-61
Liberal Party (England), 70
Liberalism, 37-39
Locke, John, 15, 24-25, 84
Logic (Hegel), 87
Lukacs, Georg, 34, 45, 49-63, 87
100
background and history, 50-53
opposition to Stalinism, 53-57
praxis, 57-63
socialization of work, 59-60

McCarthy, Eugene, 20-22
Majority rule
liberal democratic theory and,
23-24, 28
myth of, 87-90
Mann, Heinrich, 51
Mann, Thomas, 51
Marx, Karl, 58, 70, 81, 88, 96-97,
119, 143, 149
Capital, 59, 83-84
communist theory, 40
concepts of alienation, 120-25,
126-28, 130-31
"Economic and Philosophic
Manuscripts," 120
"Thesis on Feuerbach," 57
Marxism, Democratic, 33-45
party revolutionary praxis, 40-45
power politics, 38-39
return to, 33-34, 39-40, 45
Soviet formulation of dialectical
materialism, 34-37
See also Lukacs, Georg

Materialism, dialectical, 5, 55,
153-54
Soviet formulation of, 34-37
Means of production, 94
Mill, John Stuart, 70
Minority rights, 90-92
liberal democratic theory, 23-24,
28
Mississippi Summer (1964), 16-17,
20
Monism, 86
Movement, the, 92-93
building a revolutionary
movement, 149-64

Natural rights, 25, 90-92
New Deal, 10, 37
New democratic theory, East-West
relationship and, 7-11
New Industrial State (Galbraith),
102
New political language, *see*
Political language
Nixon, Richard, 155

Objectification of work, 123
Oppression, revolution and,
158-60
Organization
party, 43-44
revolutionary, 149
Ownership, 94-95

Party
new concepts of, 92-93
political, 25-27
revolutionary praxis, 40-45
Party organization, 43-44

Index

Index

DATE DUE

MAY 20 '7?	MAY 25 '7?		
MAY 6 '80	MAY 6 '80		
MAY 8 '80	MAY 19 '80		
GAYLORL			PRINTED IN U.S.A.